What's Your Baby's Name?

A Book to Help You Name Your Baby

Bruce Lansky

Illustrations by Jone Hallmark

Meadowbrook Press

Distributed by Simon & Schuster
New York

Library of Congress Cataloging-in-Publication Data
What's your baby's name? / Bruce Lansky
    p. cm.
  ISBN 0-88166-374-3 (Meadowbrook)
  ISBN 0-671-31864-0 (Simon & Schuster)
      1. Names, Personal—Dictionaries. I. Title.
  CS2377.L375 2000
  929.4'4'03—dc21

                                    00-039442

Managing Editor: Christine Zuchora-Walske
Copyeditor: Angela Wiechmann
Proofreader: Laurie Anderson
Production Manager: Paul Woods
Desktop Publishing: Danielle White
Cover and Interior Art: Jone Hallmark

Published by Meadowbrook Press, 5451 Smetana Drive,
Minnetonka, Minnesota 55343

www.meadowbrookpress.com

BOOK TRADE DISTRIBUTION by Simon & Schuster, a division of
Simon and Schuster, Inc., 1230 Avenue of the Americas, New
York, NY 10020

03 02 01 00   12 11 10 9 8 7 6 5 4 3 2 1

Printed in China

Girls'
Names

Abby, Abbey, Abbie
(Hebrew) familiar forms
of Abigail.

Abigail (Hebrew) father's
joy.

Ada (German) a short form
of Adelaide. (English)
prosperous; happy.

Addie (Greek, German)
a familiar form of
Adelaide, Adrienne.

Adelaide (German) noble
and serene.

Adele (German, English) a
short form of Adelaide,
Adeline.

Adeline (English) a form of
Adelaide.

Adina (Hebrew) noble;
adorned.

Adriana, Adrianna (Italian)
forms of Adrienne.

Adriane, Adrianne
(English) forms of
Adrienne.

Adrienne (Greek) rich.
(Latin) dark. A feminine
form of Adrian.

Afton (English) from Afton,
England.

Agatha (Greek) good;
kind.

Agnes (Greek) pure.

Aileen (Scottish) light
bearer. (Irish) a form
of Helen.

Aimee (Latin) an alternate
form of Amy. (French)
loved.

Ainsley (Scottish) my own
meadow.

Aisha, Asha (Swahili) life.
(Arabic) woman.

Aja (Hindi) goat.

Alaina, Alayna (Irish)
alternate forms of Alana.

Alana (Irish) attractive;
peaceful. (Hawaiian)
offering. A feminine
form of Alan.

Alea, Aleah (Arabic) high; exalted. (Persian) God's being.

Alecia (Greek) a form of Alicia.

Alejandra (Spanish) a form of Alexandra.

Alena (Russian) a form of Helen.

Alesha (Greek) an alternate form of Alecia, Alisha.

Alessandra (Italian) a form of Alexandra.

Alex, Alexa (Greek) short forms of Alexandra.

Alexandra, Alexandria (Greek) defender of mankind. Feminine forms of Alexander.

Alexia, Alexis (Greek) short forms of Alexandra.

Ali, Allie (Greek) familiar forms of Alice, Alicia, Alison.

Alia, Aliya (Hebrew) ascender.

Alice (Greek) truthful. (German) noble.

Alicia, Alycia (English) alternate forms of Alice.

Alida (Latin) small and winged. (Spanish) noble.

Alina, Aline (Slavic) bright. (Scottish) fair. (English) short forms of Adeline.

Alisa, Alissa (Greek) alternate forms of Alice.

Alisha (Greek) truthful. (German) noble. (English) an alternate form of Alicia.

Alison, Allison, Allyson, Alyson (English) forms of Alice.

Alix (Greek) a short form of Alexandra, Alice.

Aliza (Hebrew) joyful.

Alma (Arabic) learned. (Latin) soul.

Alysa, Alyse, Alysse (Greek) alternate forms of Alice.

Alysha, Alysia (Greek) alternate forms of Alisha.

Alyssa (Greek) rational.

Amanda (Latin) lovable.

Amaris (Hebrew) promised by God.

Amber (French) amber.

Amelia (Latin) an alternate form of Emily. (German) hardworking.

Amelie (German) a familiar form of Amelia.

Amina (Arabic) trustworthy; faithful.

Amy (Latin) beloved.

Ana (Hawaiian, Spanish) a form of Hannah.

Anais (Hebrew) gracious.

Anastasia (Greek) resurrection.

Andrea (Greek) strong; courageous. (Latin) feminine. A feminine form of Andrew.

Angel (Greek) a short form of Angela.

Angela (Greek) angel; messenger.

Angelica (Greek) an alternate form of Angela.

Angelina, Angeline (Russian) forms of Angela.

Angelique (French) a form of Angela.

Angie (Greek) a familiar form of Angela.

Anika (Czech) a familiar form of Anna.

Anisha (English) a form of Agnes, Ann.

Anita (Spanish) a form of Ann, Anna.

Ann, Anne (English) forms of Hannah.

Anna (German, Italian, Czech, Swedish) a form of Hannah.

Annemarie, Anne-Marie, Annmarie (English) combinations of Ann + Marie.

Annette (French) a form of Ann.

Annie (English) a familiar form of Ann.

Annik, Annika (Russian) forms of Ann.

Antoinette (French) a form of Antonia.

Antonia (Greek) flourishing. (Latin) praiseworthy. A feminine form of Anthony.

Anya (Russian) a form of Anna.

April, Apryl (Latin) opening.

Arabella (Latin) beautiful altar.

Aretha (Greek) virtuous.

Ariana, Arianna (Greek) holy.

Ariane (French) form of Ariana.

Arianne (English) a form of Ariana.

Ariel (Hebrew) lioness of God.

Arielle (French) a form of Ariel.

Arin (Hebrew) enlightened. (Arabic) messenger. A feminine form of Aaron.

Arlene (Irish) pledge. A feminine form of Arlen.

Ashley (English) ash-tree meadow.

Ashlyn, Ashlynn (English) ash-tree pool. (Irish) vision; dream.

Asia (Greek) resurrection. (English) eastern sunrise. (Swahili) an alternate form of Aisha.

Aspen (English) aspen tree.

Athena (Greek) wise.

Aubrey (German) noble; bearlike. (French) blond ruler; elf ruler.

Aubrie (French) an alternate form of Aubrey.

Audrey (English) noble strength.

Aurora (Latin) dawn.

Autumn (Latin) autumn.

Ava (Greek) an alternate form of Eva.

Ayanna (Hindi) innocent.

Ayesha (Persian) a form of Aisha.

Ayla (Hebrew) oak tree.

Bailey (English) bailiff.

Bandi (Punjabi) prisoner.

Barbara (Latin) stranger, foreigner.

Beatrice (Latin) blessed; happy; bringer of joy.

Becky (American) a familiar form of Rebecca.

Belinda (Spanish) beautiful.

Belle (French) beautiful. A short form of Belinda, Isabel.

Benita (Spanish) blessed.

Bernadette (French) brave as a bear. (English) a feminine form of Bernard.

Bertha (German) bright; illustrious; brilliant ruler.

Beth (Hebrew, Aramaic) house of God. A short form of Bethany, Elizabeth.

Bethany (Aramaic) house of figs.

Betsy (American) a familiar form of Elizabeth.

Bettina (American) a combination of Beth + Tina.

Betty (Hebrew) consecrated to God. (English) a familiar form of Elizabeth.

Beverly (English) beaver field.

Bianca, Blanca (Italian) white.

Billie (English) strong willed.

Blair (Scottish) plains dweller.

Blythe (English) happy, cheerful.

Bobbi, Bobbie (American) familiar forms of Barbara, Roberta.

Bobbi-Jo (American) a combination of Bobbi + Jo.

Bonita (Spanish) pretty.

Bonnie, Bonny (English, Scottish) beautiful, pretty. (Spanish) familiar forms of Bonita.

Brandy, Brandi, Brandie (Dutch) an after-dinner drink made from distilled wine.

Briana, Brianne, Breanna, Bryanne (Irish) strong; virtuous; honorable. Feminine forms of Brian.

Bree (Irish) a short form of Breanna. (English) broth.

Brenda (Irish) little raven. (English) sword. A feminine form of Brendan.

Brenna (Irish) an alternate form of Brenda.

Brett (Irish) a short form of Brittany.

Briar (French) heather.

Bridget, Bridgett, Bridgette (Irish) strong.

Brie (French) a type of cheese.

Brieanne (American) a combination of Brie + Ann.

Brielle (French) a form of Brie.

Brienne (French) a form of Briana.

Brigitte (French) a form of Bridget.

Britt, Britta (Latin) short forms of Brittany. (Swedish) strong.

Brittany, Britaney, Britany, Britney (English) from Great Britain.

Bronwyn (Welsh) white breasted.

Brooke (English) brook, stream.

Bryn, Brynn (Latin) from the boundary line. (Welsh) mound.

Cailin (American) a form of Caitlin.

Caitlin, Caitlyn (Irish) alternate forms of Cathleen.

Calandra (Greek) lark.

Caleigh, Caley (American) alternate forms of Kayley, Kelly.

Cali, Calli (Greek) alternate forms of Callie.

Callie (Greek, Arabic) beautiful.

Calvina (Latin) bald. A feminine form of Calvin.

Cameron (Scottish) crooked nose.

Cami, Cammie (French) short forms of Camille.

Camilla (Italian) a form of Camille.

Camille (French) young ceremonial attendant.

Candace, Candice, Candis, Candyce (Greek) glittering white; glowing.

Candra (Latin) glowing.

Candy, Candi (American) familiar forms of Candace.

Caprice (Italian) fanciful.

Cara (Latin) dear. (Irish) friend.

Carey, Cari, Carie (Welsh) familiar forms of Cara, Caroline, Karen, Katherine.

Carina (Greek) a familiar form of Cora. (Italian) dear little one. (Swedish) a form of Karen.

Carissa (Greek) beloved.

Carla (Latin) an alternate form of Carol, Caroline. (German) farmer. (English) strong and womanly.

Carlene (English) a form of Caroline.

Carlin, Carlyn (Latin) short forms of Caroline. (Irish) little champion.

Carly, Carlee, Carli, Carlie (English) familiar forms of Caroline, Charlotte.

Carmela, Carmella (Hebrew) garden; vineyard.

Carmen (Latin) song.

Carol (German) farmer. (French) song of joy. (English) strong and womanly. A feminine form of Carl, Charles.

Carole (English) an alternate form of Carol.

Carolina (Italian) a form of Caroline.

Caroline (French) little and womanly.

Carolyn (English) a form of Caroline.

Carra (Irish) an alternate form of Cara.

Carrie (English) a familiar form of Carol, Caroline.

Caryn (Danish) a form of Karen.

Casey, Casie (Irish) brave.

Cassandra (Greek) helper of men.

Cassidy (Irish) clever.

Cassie (Greek) a familiar form of Cassandra, Catherine.

Catalina (Spanish) a form of Catherine.

Catherine (Greek) pure. (English) a form of Katherine.

Cathleen (Irish) a form of Catherine.

Cathrine, Cathryn (Greek) alternate forms of Catherine.

Cathy, Cathi (Greek) familiar forms of Catherine, Cathleen.

Catrina (Slavic) a form of Catherine, Katrina.

Cayla (Hebrew) an alternate form of Kayla.

Cecilia (Latin) blind. A feminine form of Cecil.

Celena, Celina (Greek) alternate forms of Selena.

Celeste (Latin) celestial; heavenly.

Celia (Latin) a short form of Cecilia.

Celine (Greek) an alternate form of Celena.

Chanda (Sanskrit) great goddess.

Chandra (Sanskrit) moon.

Chanel, Chanell, Chanelle (English) channel.

Chantal, Chantel, Chantelle (French) song.

Chardae, Charde (Punjabi) charitable.

Charis (Greek) grace; kindness.

Charissa, Charisse (Greek) forms of Charity.

Charity (Latin) charity, kindness.

Charla (French, English) a short form of Charlene, Charlotte.

Charlene (English) a form of Caroline.

Charlie (German, English) strong and womanly. A feminine form of Charles.

Charlotte (French) a form of Caroline.

Charmaine (French) a form of Carmen.

Chastity, Chasity, Chassidy (Latin) pure.

Chelsea, Chelsey, Chelsie (English) seaport.

Cherie, Cheri (French) familiar forms of Cheryl.

Cherise (French) a form of Cherish.

Cherish (English) dearly held, precious.

Cheryl, Cherelle, Cherrelle (French) beloved.

Cheyenne (Cheyenne) a tribal name.

Chiquita (Spanish) little one.

Chloe (Greek) blooming; verdant.

Chrissy, Christy, Cristy (English) familiar forms of Christina.

Christa (German) a short form of Christina.

Christal (Latin) an alternate form of Crystal. (Scottish) a form of Christina.

Christen, Christin (Greek) alternate forms of Christina.

Christian, Christiana (Greek) alternate forms of Christina.

Christie, Christi (Greek) short forms of Christina, Christine.

Christina, Cristina (Greek) Christian; anointed.

Christine (French, English) a form of Christina.

Ciara, Cierra (Irish) black.

Cindy (Greek) moon. (Latin) a familiar form of Cynthia.

Claire (French) a form of Clara.

Clara (Latin) clear; bright.

Clare (English) a form of Clara.

Clarissa (Greek) brilliant. (Italian) a form of Clara.

Claudia (Latin) lame. A feminine form of Claude.

Cody, Codi (English) cushion.

Colby (English) coal town.

Coleen, Colleen (Irish) girl.

Colette (Greek, French) a familiar form of Nicole.

Connie (Latin) a familiar form of Constance.

Constance (Latin) constant; firm.

Cora (Greek) maiden.

Coral (Latin) coral.

Corey, Cory (Greek) familiar forms of Cora. (Irish) from the hollow.

Corie, Cori, Corrie (Irish) alternate forms of Corey.

Corina, Corinna (Greek) familiar forms of Corinne.

Corinne (Greek) maiden.

Corissa (Greek) a familiar form of Cora.

Courtney, Cortney, Courtenay (English) from the court.

Crista (Italian) a form of Christa.

Cristen, Cristin (Irish) forms of Christen.

Crystal (Latin) clear, brilliant glass.

Cynthia (Greek) moon.

Daisy (English) day's eye.

Dakota (Dakota) tribal name.

Dale (English) valley.

Dallas (Irish) wise.

Damaris (Greek) gentle girl.

Dana (English) from Denmark; bright as da'

Danae (Greek) the mother of Perseus in mythology.

Danelle (Hebrew) an alternate form of Danielle.

Danette (American) a form of Danielle.

Dani, Dania, Danya (Hebrew) short forms of Danielle.

Danica, Danika (Hebrew) alternate forms of Danielle. (Slavic) morning star.

Daniella (Italian) a form of Danielle.

Danielle (Hebrew, French) God is my judge. A feminine form of Daniel.

Danna (Hebrew) a short form of Daniella. (English) an alternate form of Dana.

Danyel, Danyell (American) forms of Danielle.

Daphne (Greek) laurel tree.

Dara (Hebrew) compassionate.

Darby (Irish) free. (Scandinavian) deer estate.

Darcy, Darci (Irish) dark. (French) fortress.

Daria (Greek) wealthy. A feminine form of Darius.

Darla (English) a short form of Darlene.

Darlene (French) little darling.

Daryl (French) a short form of Darlene. (English) beloved.

Davina (Hebrew) beloved.

Dawn, Dawna (English) sunrise, dawn.

Dayna (Scandinavian) a form of Dana.

Deana, Deanna, Deanne (Latin) divine. (English) valley. Feminine forms of Dean.

Deandra (American) a combination of prefix De + Andrea.

Debbie (Hebrew) a short form of Deborah.

Deborah (Hebrew) bee.

Debra (American) a short form of Deborah.

Dedra (American) a form of Deirdre.

Deena (American) a form of Deana, Dena.

Deirdre, Deidra, Deidre (Irish) sorrowful; wanderer.

Delia (Greek) visible; from Delos, Greece. (German, Welsh) a short form of Adelaide.

Delilah (Hebrew) brooder.

Della a short form of Adelaide.

Demetria (Greek) lover of the earth.

Demi (Greek) a short form of Demetria. (French) half.

Dena (Hebrew) an alternate form of Dina. (English, Native American) valley.

Denae (Hebrew) an alternate form of Dena.

Denise (French) follower of Dionysus, the god of wine. A feminine form of Dennis.

Denisha (American) a form of Denise.

Desiree (French) desired, longed for.

Destiny (French) fate.

Devin (Irish) poet. An alternate form of Devon.

Devon (English) from Devonshire, England.

Diamond (Latin) precious gem.

Diana, Diane, Dianna
(Latin) divine.

Dina (Hebrew) vindicated.

Dionne (Greek) divine queen.

Dixie (French) tenth. (English) wall; dike.

Dolores, Delores (Spanish) sorrowful.

Dominique, Domonique (French) belonging to the Lord.

Donna (Italian) lady.

Dora (Greek) gift.

Doreen (Greek) an alternate form of Dora. (Irish) moody; sullen. (French) golden.

Doris (Greek) sea.

Dorothy (Greek) gift of God.

Drew (Greek) courageous; strong.

Dusty (German) valiant fighter. (English) brown rock quarry. A feminine form of Dustin.

Ebony, Eboni, Ebonie
(Greek) a hard, dark wood.

Echo (Greek) repeated sound.

Eden (Babylonian) a plain. (Hebrew) delightful.

Edith (English) rich gift.

Edna (Hebrew) rejuvenation.

Eileen (Irish) a form of Helen.

Elaine (French) a form of Helen.

Elana (Greek) a short form of Eleanor.

Eleanor (Greek) an alternate form of Helen.

Elena (Greek) an alternate form of Eleanor. (Italian) a form of Helen.

Eliana (Hebrew) my God has answered me. A feminine form of Eli, Elijah.

Elicia (Hebrew) an alternate form of Elisha.

Elisa (Spanish, Italian, English) a short form of Elizabeth.

Elise (French, English) a short form of Elizabeth, Elyse.

Elisha (Greek) an alternate form of Alisha. (Hebrew) consecrated to God.

Elissa, Elyssa (Greek, English) forms of Elizabeth. Short forms of Melissa.

Eliza (Hebrew) a short form of Elizabeth.

Elizabeth (Hebrew) consecrated to God.

Elle, Ella (Greek) short forms of Eleanor. (English) elfin; beautiful fairy-woman.

Ellen (English) a form of Eleanor, Helen.

Elsa (Hebrew) a short form of Elizabeth. (German) noble.

Elsie (German) a familiar form of Elsa.

Elyse, Elysia (Latin) sweet; blissful.

Emerald (French) bright green gemstone.

Emilee, Emilie (English) forms of Emily.

Emilia (Italian) a form of Amelia, Emily.

Emily (Latin) flatterer. (German) industrious. A feminine form of Emil.

Emma (German) a short form of Emily.

Erica (Scandinavian) ruler of all. (English) brave ruler. A feminine form of Eric.

Erin (Irish) peace.

Estelle (French) a form of Esther.

Esther (Persian) star.

Eugenia (Greek) born to nobility. A feminine form of Eugene.

Eunice (Greek) happy; victorious.

Eva (Greek) a short form of Evangelina. (Hebrew) an alternate form of Eve.

Evangelina (Greek) bearer of good news.

Eve (Hebrew) life.

Evelyn (English) hazelnut.

Evette (French) an alternate form of Yvette.

Evie (Hungarian) a form of Eve.

Faith (English) faithfulness, fidelity.

Fallon (Irish) grandchild of the ruler.

Fannie (American) a familiar form of Frances.

Farah, Farrah (English) beautiful; pleasant.

Faren, Farren (English) wanderer.

Fatima (Arabic) daughter of the Prophet.

Fawn (French) young deer.

Faye (French) fairy; elf. (English) an alternate form of Faith.

Felica (Spanish) a short form of Felicia.

Felicia, Felecia, Felisha (Latin) fortunate; happy. Feminine forms of Felix.

Fiona (Irish) fair; white.

Flora (Latin) flower. A short form of Florence.

Florence (Latin) blooming; flowery; prosperous.

Frances (Latin) free; from France. A feminine form of Francis.

Francesca, Franchesca (Italian) forms of Frances.

Francine (French) a form of Frances.

Frankie (American) a familiar form of Frances.

Gabriela, Gabriella (Italian) alternate forms of Gabrielle.

Gabrielle (French) devoted to God. A feminine form of Gabriel.

Gail (Hebrew) a short form of Abigail. (English) merry, lively.

Gayle (English) an alternate form of Gail.

Gemma (Latin, Italian) jewel, precious stone.

Gena (French) a form of Gina. A short form of Geneva, Genevieve.

Geneva (French) juniper tree. A short form of Genevieve.

Genevieve (French, Welsh) white wave; white phantom.

Genna (English) a form of Jenna.

Georgette (French) a form of Georgia.

Georgia (Greek) farmer. A feminine form of George.

Georgina (English) a form of Georgia.

Geraldine (German) mighty with a spear. A feminine form of Gerald.

Geri (American) a familiar form of Geraldine.

Gianna (Italian) a short form of Giovanna.

Gillian (Latin) an alternate form of Jillian.

Gina (Italian) a short form of Angelina, Eugenia, Regina, Virginia.

Ginger (Latin) flower; spice. A familiar form of Virginia.

Ginny (English) a familiar form of Ginger, Virginia.

Giovanna (Italian) a form of Jane.

Giselle (German) pledge; hostage.

Gladys (Latin) small sword. (Irish) princess. (Welsh) a form of Claudia.

Glenda (Welsh) a form of Glenna.

Glenna (Irish) valley, glen. A feminine form of Glenn.

Gloria (Latin) glory.

Grace (Latin) graceful.

Greta (German) a short form of Gretchen, Margaret.

Gretchen (German) a form of Margaret.

Guadalupe (Arabic) river of black stones.

Gurpreet (Punjabi) religion.

Gwen (Welsh) a short form of Gwendolyn.

Gwendolyn (Welsh) white wave; white browed; new moon.

Haiden, Hayden (English) heather-covered hill.

Haley, Hallie (Scandinavian) heroine.

Hana (Japanese) flower. (Arabic) happiness. (Slavic) a form of Hannah.

Hannah, Hanna (Hebrew) gracious.

Harmony (Latin) harmonious.

Harpreet (Punjabi) devoted to God.

Harriet (French) ruler of the household. (English) an alternate form of Henrietta.

Hasana (Swahili) she arrived first.

Hayley, Hailey (English) hay meadow.

Hazel (English) hazelnut tree; commanding authority.

Heather (English) flowering heather.

Heaven (English) place of beauty and happiness.

Hedda (German) battler.

Heidi (German) a short form of Adelaide.

Helen, Helena (Greek) light.

Helene (French) a form of Helen.

Helki (Native American) touched.

Heloise (French) a form of Louise.

Henrietta (English) ruler of the household. A feminine form of Henry.

Hilary, Hillary (Greek) cheerful, merry.

Holly, Holley, Holli, Hollie (English) holly tree.

Hope (English) hope.

Ida (German) hardworking. (English) prosperous.

Iesha (American) a form of Aisha.

Ikia (Hebrew) God is my salvation. (Hawaiian) a feminine form of Isaiah.

Ilana (Hebrew) tree.

India (Hindi) from India.

Ingrid (Scandinavian) hero's daughter; beautiful daughter.

Irene (Greek) peaceful.

Iris (Greek) rainbow.

Isabel (Spanish) a form of Elizabeth.

Isabelle (French) a form of Isabel.

Ivette (French) an alternate form of Yvette.

Ivory (Latin) made of ivory.

Ivy (English) ivy tree.

Jacalyn, Jacklyn, Jaclyn, (American) forms of Jacqueline.

Jacey (Greek) a familiar form of Jacinda. (American) a combination of the initials J. + C.

Jacinda, Jacinta (Greek) beautiful, attractive.

Jackie, Jacki (American) familiar forms of Jacqueline.

Jacqueline, Jackqueline, Jacquelyn, Jacquelynn (French) supplanter; substitute. Feminine forms of Jacques.

Jade (Spanish) jade.

Jaime, Jaimee (French) I love.

Jami, Jamie (Hebrew) supplanter; substitute. (English) feminine forms of James.

Jamila (Arabic) beautiful.

Jamilynn (English) a combination of Jami + Lynn.

Jammie (American) a form of Jami.

Jan (English) a short form of Jane, Janet, Janice.

Jana (Slavic) a form of Jane.

Janae, Janay (American) forms of Jane.

Jane (Hebrew) God is gracious. A feminine form of John.

Janelle, Janel, Janell (French) forms of Jane.

Janessa (American) a form of Jane.

Janet (English) a form of Jane.

Janice (Hebrew) God is gracious. (English) a familiar form of Jane.

Janie (English) a familiar form of Jane.

Janine (French) a form of Jane.

Janis (English) a form of Jane.

Janna (Hebrew) a short form of Johana. (Arabic) harvest of fruit.

Jasmine, Jazmin, Jazmine (Persian) jasmine flower.

Jaspreet (Punjabi) virtuous.

Jaye (Latin) jaybird.

Jaylene (American) a form of Jaye.

Jayme, Jaymie (English) alternate forms of Jami.

Jayna (Hebrew) an alternate form of Jane.

Jayne (Hindi) victorious. (English) a form of Jane.

Jean, Jeana, Jeanna, Jeanne (Scottish) forms of Jane, Joan.

Jeanette (French) a form of Jean.

Jeanie (Scottish) a familiar form of Jean.

Jeanine, Jenine (Scottish) alternate forms of Jean.

Jena (Arabic) an alternate form of Jenna.

Jenelle (American) a combination of Jenny + Nell.

Jenilee (American) a combination of Jenny + Lee.

Jenna (Arabic) small bird. (Welsh) a short form of Jennifer.

Jennica (Romanian) a form of Jane.

Jennifer, Jenifer, Jeniffer (Welsh) white wave; white phantom.

Jenny, Jenni, Jennie (Welsh) familiar forms of Jennifer.

Jeraldine (English) a form of Geraldine.

Jeri, Jerri, Jerrie (American) short forms of Jeraldine.

Jerica (American) a combination of Jeri + Erica.

Jerilyn (American) a combination of Jeri + Lynn.

Jessalyn (American) a combination of Jessica + Lynn.

Jessenia (Arabic) flower.

Jessica, Jessika (Hebrew) wealthy. Feminine forms of Jesse.

Jessie, Jesse, Jessi (Hebrew) short forms of Jessica. (Scottish) a form of Janet.

Jill (English) a short form of Jillian.

Jillian (Latin) an alternate form of Julia.

Jo (American) a short form of Joanna, Jolene, Josephine.

Joan (Hebrew) an alternate form of Jane.

Joanie (Hebrew) a familiar form of Joan.

Joanna, Joanne (English) forms of Joan.

Jocelyn, Joselyn, Joslyn (Latin) joyous.

Jody, Jodi, Jodie (American) familiar forms of Judith.

Joelle (Hebrew) God is willing. A feminine form of Joel.

Johana, Johanna (German) forms of Joanna.

Johnna, Jonna (American) forms of Joanna, Johana.

Joleen, Joline (English) alternate forms of Jolene.

Jolene (Hebrew) God will add, God will increase. (English) a form of Josephine.

Jonelle (American) a combination of Joan + Elle.

Joni (American) a familiar form of Joan.

Jordan, Jordana, Jordanna (Hebrew) descending.

Josee (American) familiar forms of Josephine.

Josephine (French) God will add, God will increase. A feminine form of Joseph.

Josie (Hebrew) a familiar form of Josephine.

Joy (Latin) joyous.

Joyce (Latin) a short form of Jocelyn.

Juanita (Spanish) a form of Jane, Joan.

Judith (Hebrew) praised.

Judy (Hebrew) a familiar form of Judith.

Julia (Latin) youthful. A feminine form of Julius.

Juliana (Czech, Spanish) a form of Julia.

Juliann, Julianne (English) forms of Julia.

Julianna (Hungarian) a form of Julia.

Julie (English) a form of Julia.

Juliet, Juliette (French) forms of Julia.

June (Latin) born in the sixth month.

Justina (Italian) a form of Justine.

Justine (Latin) just; righteous. A feminine form of Justin.

Kacey, Kacy, Kasey, Kasie (Irish) brave. (American) alternate forms of Casey. Combinations of the initials K. + C.

Kaci, Kacie, Kaycee (American) alternate forms of Kacey.

Kady (English) an alternate form of Katy. A combination of the initials K. + D.

Kaela (Hebrew, Arabic) beloved, sweetheart.

Kaelyn (American) a combination of Kaela + Lynn.

Kaila (Hebrew) laurel; crown.

Kaitlin, Kaitlyn, Katelin, Katelyn (Irish) alternate forms of Caitlin.

Kala (Arabic) a short form of Kaila.

Kaleena (Hawaiian) pure.

Kali (Sanskrit) energy; black goddess; time the destroyer. (Hawaiian) hesitating.

Kallie, Kalli (Greek) alternate forms of Callie.

Kalyn, Kaylin, Kaylyn (American) combinations of Kay + Lynn.

Kami (Italian, North African) a short form of Kamilah. (Japanese) divine aura.

Kamilah (North African) perfect.

Kandace, Kandice (Greek) glittering white; glowing. (American) alternate forms of Candace.

Kara (Greek, Danish) an alternate form of Katherine.

Karah (Greek, Danish) an alternate form of Kara. (Irish, Italian) an alternate form of Cara.

Karen (Greek) an alternate form of Katherine.

Kari (Greek) pure. (Danish) a form of Caroline, Katherine.

Karin (Scandinavian) a form of Karen.

Karina, Karine (Russian) forms of Karen.

Karissa (Greek) an alternate form of Carissa.

Karla (German) an alternate form of Carla.

Karly, Karli (Latin) little and womanly. (American) forms of Carly.

Karmen (Hebrew) a form of Carmen.

Karolyn (American) a form of Carolyn.

Karrie, Karri (American) forms of Carrie.

Karyn (American) a form of Karen.

Kasi (Hindi) from the holy city.

Kassandra (Greek) an alternate form of Cassandra.

Kassidy (Irish) clever. (American) an alternate form of Cassidy.

Kassie, Kassi (American) familiar forms of Kassandra, Kassidy.

Katarina (Czech) a form of Katherine.

Kate (Greek) pure. (English) a short form of Katherine.

Katherine, Katharine (Greek) pure.

Kathleen (Irish) a form of Katherine.

Kathrine (English) a form of Katherine.

Kathy, Kathi (English) familiar forms of Katherine, Kathleen.

Katlyn (Greek) pure. (Irish) an alternate form of Kaitlin.

Katrina (German) a form of Katherine.

Katy (English) a familiar form of Kate.

Kay (Greek) rejoicer. (Teutonic) a fortified place. (Latin) merry. A short form of Katherine.

Kayla (Arabic, Hebrew) an alternate form of Kaela.

Kayleen, Kaylene (Hebrew) alternate forms of Kayla.

Kayley, Kailee, Kailey, Kayleigh (American) familiar forms of Kaila.

Keara (Irish) dark; black.

Keeley, Keely (Irish) alternate forms of Kelly.

Keena (Irish) brave.

Keira, Kiara (Irish) little and dark. A feminine form of Kieran.

Keisha, Keshia (American) forms of Aisha.

Kelly, Kelley, Kelli, Kellie (Irish) brave warrior.

Kellyn (Irish) a combination of Kelly + Lyn.

Kelsey (Scandinavian, Scottish) ship island. (English) an alternate form of Chelsea.

Kelsie, Kelsi (Scottish) forms of Chelsea.

Kendall (English) ruler of the valley.

Kendra (English) water baby. (Dakota) magical power.

Kenna (Irish) beautiful. A feminine form of Kenneth.

Kenya (Hebrew) animal's horn.

Kenzie (Scottish) light skinned. (Irish) a short form of Mackenzie.

Kera (Irish) a short form of Kerry.

Keren (Hebrew) animal's horn.

Kerry, Kerri, Kerrie (Irish) dark haired.

Khadijah (Arabic) trustworthy.

Kia (African) season's beginning. (American) a short form of Kiana.

Kiana (American) a combination of the prefix Ki + Anna.

Kiera, Kierra (Irish) alternate forms of Kerry.

Kiley (Irish) attractive; from the straits.

Kim (Vietnamese) needle. (English) a short form of Kimberly.

Kimberly, Kimberlee, Kimberley, Kymberly (English) chief; ruler.

Kinsey (English) offspring; relative.

Kira (Persian) sun. (Latin) light. A feminine form of Cyrus.

Kirsta (Scandinavian) an alternate form of Kirsten.

Kirsten (Greek) Christian; anointed. (Scandinavian) a form of Christine.

Kirstin (Scandinavian) an alternate form of Kirsten.

Kita (Japanese) north.

Kori (American) a form of Corey.

Kortney (English) an alternate form of Courtney.

Kourtney (American) a form of Courtney.

Krista (Czech) a form of Christina.

Kristen (Greek) Christian; anointed. (Scandinavian) a form of Christine.

Kristian, Kristiana (Greek) alternate forms of Christian.

Kristie, Kristi (Scandinavian) short forms of Kristine.

Kristin (Scandinavian) an alternate form of Kristen.

Kristina (Greek) Christian; anointed. (Scandinavian) a form of Christina.

Kristine (Scandinavian) a form of Christine.

Kristy (American) a familiar form of Kristine, Krystal.

Krysta (Polish) a form of Krista.

Krystal, Krystle (American) forms of Crystal.

Krystina (Czech) a form of Kristin.

Kyla (Irish) attractive. (Yiddish) crown; laurel.

Kyle (Irish) attractive.

Kylee (Irish) a familiar form of Kyle.

Kylene (Irish) an alternate form of Kyle.

Kylie (West Australian Aboriginal) curled stick; boomerang. (Irish) a familiar form of Kyle.

Kyra (Greek) ladylike.

Lacey, Lacy (Greek) familiar forms of Larissa. (Latin) cheerful.

Ladonna (American) a combination of the prefix La + Donna.

Laila (Arabic) an alternate form of Leila.

Laine (French) a short form of Elaine.

Lakeisha, Lakesha, Lakeshia, Lakisha (American) combinations of the prefix La + Keisha.

Lakendra (American) a combination of the prefix La + Kendra.

Lakia (Arabic) found treasure.

Lana (Latin) woolly. (Irish) attractive; peaceful. A short form of Alana, Elana. (Hawaiian) floating, buoyant.

Lani (Hawaiian) sky; heaven. A short form of Leilani.

Laquisha (American) a combination of the prefix La + Queisha.

Laquita (American) a combination of the prefix La + Quintana.

Lara (Greek) cheerful. (Latin) shining; famous.

Larissa (Greek) cheerful.

Lashanda (American) a combination of the prefix La + Shanda.

Lashawna (American) a combination of the prefix La + Shana.

Lashonda (American) a combination of the prefix La + Shonda.

Latanya (American) a combination of the prefix La + Tanya.

Latara (American) a combination of the prefix La + Tara.

Latasha (American) a combination of the prefix La + Tasha.

Latavia (American) a combination of the prefix La + Tavia.

Latesha (American) a form of Leticia.

Latia (American) a combination of the prefix La + Tia.

Latisha (Latin) an alternate form of Leticia.

Latonya (American) a combination of the prefix La + Tonya.

Latoria (American) a combination of the prefix La + Tori.

Latosha (American) a combination of the prefix La + Tosha.

Latoya (American) a combination of the prefix La + Toya.

Latrice (American) a combination of the prefix La + Trice.

Latricia (American) a combination of the prefix La + Tricia.

Laura (Latin) crowned with laurel. A feminine form of Laurence.

Laurel (Latin) laurel tree.

Lauren (English) a form of Laura.

Laurie (English) a familiar form of Laura.

Lawanda (American) a combination of the prefix La + Wanda.

Layla (Hebrew, Arabic) an alternate form of Leila.

Lea (Hawaiian) the goddess of canoe makers.

Leah (Hebrew) weary.

Leandra (Latin) like a lioness.

Leanne, Lean (English) forms of Leeann.

Lee (Chinese) plum. (Irish) poetic. (English) meadow. A short form of Ashley, Leah.

Leeann, Leeanne (English) combinations of Lee + Ann.

Leigh (English) an alternate form of Lee.

Leila (Hebrew) dark beauty; night. (Arabic) born at night.

Leilani (Hawaiian) heavenly flower; heavenly child.

Lena (Greek) a short form of Eleanor. (Hebrew) dwelling, lodging. (Latin) temptress. (Norwegian) illustrious.

Leona (German) brave as a lioness. A feminine form of Leon.

Lesley, Leslie (Scottish) gray fortress.

Leticia (Latin) joy.

Lia (Greek) bringer of good news. (Hebrew, Dutch, Italian) dependent.

Liana (Hebrew) a short form of Eliana. (Latin) youth. (French) bound, wrapped up; tree covered with vines. (English) meadow.

Liane, Lianne (Hebrew) alternate forms of Liana.

Liberty (Latin) free.

Lidia (Greek) an alternate form of Lydia.

Lila (Arabic) night. (Hindi) free will of god. (Persian) lilac. A short form of Delilah, Lillian.

Lillian (Latin) lily flower.

Lily (Latin, Arabic) a familiar form of Lillian.

Lina (Greek) light. (Latin) an alternate form of Lena. (Arabic) tender.

Linda (Spanish) pretty.

Lindsay, Lindsey, Linsey (English) linden-tree island; camp near the stream.

Lindsi (American) a familiar form of Lindsay.

Linette, Lynnette (Welsh) idol. (French) bird.

Linnea (Scandinavian) lime tree.

Lisa (Hebrew) consecrated to God. (English) a short form of Elizabeth.

Lise (German) a form of Lisa.

Lisette (French) a form of Lisa. (English) a familiar form of Elise, Elizabeth.

Liza (American) a short form of Elizabeth.

Lois (German) an alternate form of Louise.

Lola (Spanish) a familiar form of Dolores, Louise.

Loni (English) solitary.

Lora (Latin) crowned with laurel. (American) a form of Laura.

Loren (American) an alternate form of Lauren.

Lorena (English) an alternate form of Lauren.

Loretta (English) a familiar form of Laura.

Lori (Latin) crowned with laurel. (French) a short form of Lorraine, France. (American) a familiar form of Laura.

Lorna (Latin) an alternate form of Laura.

Lorraine (Latin) sorrowful. (French) from Lorraine.

Louisa (English) a familiar form of Louise.

Louise (German) famous warrior. A feminine form of Louis.

Lucia (Italian, Spanish) a form of Lucy.

Lucie (French) a familiar form of Lucy.

Lucille (English) a familiar form of Lucy.

Lucinda (Latin) a familiar form of Lucy.

Lucy (Latin) light; bringer of light.

Luisa (Spanish) a form of Louisa.

Luz (Spanish) light.

Lydia (Greek) from Lydia, an ancient land once ruled by Midas. (Arabic) strife.

Lynda (Spanish) pretty. (American) a form of Linda.

Lyndsay (American) a form of Lindsay.

Lyndsey (English) linden-tree island; camp near the stream. (American) a form of Lindsay.

Lynn, Lynne (English) waterfall; pool below a waterfall.

Lynsey (American) an alternate form of Lyndsay.

Mabel (Latin) lovable.

Mackenzie (Irish) daughter of the wise leader.

Madeleine (French) a form of Madeline.

Madeline (Greek) high tower. (English) from Magdala, England.

Madelyn (Greek) an alternate form of Madeline.

Madison (English) good; son of Maud.

Maegan (Irish) an alternate form of Megan.

Magan, Magen (Greek) short forms of Margaret.

Magdalena (Greek) high tower.

Maggie (Greek) pearl. (English) a familiar form of Magdalena, Margaret.

Maia (Greek) mother; nurse. (English) kinswoman; maiden.

Makayla (American) an alternate form of Michaela.

Malia (Hawaiian, Zuni) a form of Mary. (Spanish) a form of Maria.

Malika (Hungarian) industrious.

Mallorie (French) an alternate form of Mallory.

Mallory (German) army counselor. (French) unlucky.

Mandeep (Punjabi) enlightened.

Mandis (Xhosa) sweet.

Mandy (Latin) lovable. A familiar form of Amanda, Melinda.

Manpreet (Punjabi) mind full of love.

Mara (Greek) eternally beautiful. (Slavic) a form of Mary.

Marcella (Latin) martial, warlike.

Marcia (Latin) an alternate form of Marcella.

Marcie, Marci, Marcy (English) familiar forms of Marcella, Marcia.

Maren (Latin) sea. (Aramaic) a form of Mary.

Margaret (Greek) pearl.

Margarita (Italian, Spanish) a form of Margaret.

Margie (English) a familiar form of Margaret.

Margo, Margot (French) forms of Margaret.

Marguerite (French) a form of Margaret.

Mari (Japanese) ball. (Spanish) a form of Mary.

Maria (Hebrew) bitter; sea of bitterness. (Italian, Spanish) a form of Mary.

Mariah (Hebrew) an alternate form of Mary.

Mariana (Spanish) a form of Marian.

Maribel (French) beautiful. (English) a combination of Maria + Belle.

Marie (French) a form of Mary.

Mariel (German, Dutch) a form of Mary.

Marika (Dutch, Slavic) a form of Mary.

Marilyn (Hebrew) Mary's line or descendants.

Marina (Latin) sea.

Marion (French) a form of Mary.

Marisa, Marissa (Latin) sea.

Marisela (Latin) an alternate form of Marisa.

Marisha (Russian) a familiar form of Mary.

Marisol (Spanish) sunny sea.

Maritza (Arabic) blessed.

Marjorie (Greek) a familiar form of Margaret. (Scottish) a form of Mary.

Markita (Czech) a form of Margaret.

Marla (English) a short form of Marlena, Marlene.

Marlana (English) a form of Marlena.

Marlee, Marley (English) forms of Marlene.

Marlena (German) a form of Marlene.

Marlene (Greek) high tower. (Slavic) a form of Magdalena.

Marnie (Hebrew) a short form of Marina.

Marquita (Spanish) a form of Marcia.

Marsha (English) a form of Marcia.

Marta (English) a short form of Martha, Martina.

Martha (Aramaic) lady; sorrowful.

Martina (Latin) martial, warlike. A feminine form of Martin.

Mary (Hebrew) bitter; sea of bitterness. An alternate form of Miriam.

Maryann, Marian, Maryanne (English) combinations of Mary + Ann.

Marybeth (American) a combination of Mary + Beth.

Matty, Mattie (English) familiar forms of Martha.

Maud, Maude (English) short forms of Madeline.

Maura (Irish) an alternate form of Mary, Maureen.

Maureen (French) dark. (Irish) a form of Mary.

Maxine (Latin) greatest. A feminine form of Maximilian.

May (Latin) great. (Arabic) discerning. (English) flower; month of May.

Maya (Hindi) God's creative power. (Greek) mother; grandmother. (Latin) great. An alternate form of Maia.

McKenzie (Scottish) a form of Mackenzie.

Mead, Meade (Greek) honey wine.

Meagan (Irish) an alternate form of Megan.

Meaghan, Meghan (Welsh) forms of Megan.

Megan (Greek) pearl; great. (Irish) a form of Margaret.

Meka (Hebrew) a familiar form of Michaela.

Melanie (Greek) dark skinned.

Melina (Latin) canary yellow. (Greek) a short form of Melinda.

Melinda, Malinda (Greek) honey.

Melissa, Malissa (Greek) honey bee.

Melody (Greek) melody.

Melonie (American) an alternate form of Melanie.

Mercedes (Latin) reward; payment. (Spanish) merciful.

Meredith (Welsh) protector of the sea.

Meryl (German) famous. (Irish) shining sea. An alternate form of Muriel.

Mia (Italian) mine. A familiar form of Michaela, Michelle.

Micah (Hebrew) a short form of Michaela.

Michaela, Mikaela (Hebrew) who is like God? Feminine forms of Michael.

Michele (Italian) a form of Michaela.

Michelle (French) a form of Michaela.

Mika (Hebrew) an alternate form of Micah. (Russian) God's child. (Native American) wise raccoon.

Mila (Italian, Slavic) a short form of Camilla. (Russian) dear one.

Mildred (English) gentle counselor.

Millicent (Greek) an alternate form of Melissa. (English) industrious.

Mina (German) love. (Persian) blue sky. (Hindi) born in the lunar month of Pisces. (Arabic) harbor. (Japanese) south. A short form of names ending in "mina."

Mindy (Greek) a familiar form of Melinda.

Miranda, Maranda (Latin) strange; wonderful; admirable.

Mireille (Hebrew) God spoke. (Latin) wonderful.

Miriam, Mariam (Hebrew) bitter; sea of bitterness.

Missy (English) a familiar form of Melissa, Millicent.

Misty (English) shrouded by mist.

Moira (Irish) great. A form of Mary.

Molly (Irish) a familiar form of Mary.

Mona (Greek) a short form of Monica, Ramona. (Irish) noble.

Monica (Greek) solitary. (Latin) advisor.

Monique (French) a form of Monica.

Morgan (Welsh) seashore.

Moriah (Hebrew) God is my teacher. (French) dark skinned.

Muriel (Arabic) myrrh. (Irish) shining sea. A form of Mary.

Mylene (Greek) dark.

Myra (Latin) fragrant ointment. A feminine form of Myron.

Myriam (American) a form of Miriam.

Nada (Arabic) generous; dewy.

Nadia (French, Slavic) hopeful.

Nadine (French, Slavic) a form of Nadia.

Nakia (Arabic) pure.

Nakita (American) a form of Nicole, Nikita.

Nancy (English) gracious.

Naomi, Noemi (Hebrew) pleasant; beautiful.

Natalia (Russian) a form of Natalie.

Natalie (Latin) born on Christmas day.

Natasha (Russian) a form of Natalie.

Neila (Irish) champion. A feminine form of Neil.

Nell, Nellie (English) familiar forms of Eleanor, Helen.

Nia (Irish) a familiar form of Neila.

Nichelle (American) a combination of Nicole + Michelle.

Nicki (French) a familiar form of Nicole.

Nicola (Italian) a form of Nicole.

Nicole, Nichole, Nicolle, Nikole (French) victorious people. Feminine forms of Nicholas.

Nicolette (French) an alternate form of Nicole.

Niesha, Nisha (American) pure.

Nika (Russian) belonging to God.

Niki (Russian) a short form of Nikita.

Nikita (Russian) a form of Nicole.

Nikki (American) a familiar form of Nicole, Nikita.

Nina (Hebrew) a familiar form of Hannah. (Spanish) girl. (Native American) mighty.

Nita (Hebrew) planter. (Spanish) a short form of Anita, Juanita. (Choctaw) bear.

Noel (Latin) Christmas.

Noelle (French) a form of Noel.

Nora (Greek) a familiar form of Eleanor.

Noreen (Irish) a form of Eleanor, Nora. (Latin) a familiar form of Norma.

Nori (Japanese) law; tradition.

Norma (Latin) rule, precept.

Novella (Latin) newcomer.

Nuela (Spanish) a form of Amelia.

Nuna (Native American) land.

Nydia (Latin) nest.

Nyssa (Greek) beginning.

Oceana (Greek) ocean.

Octavia (Latin) eighth.

Olga (Scandinavian) holy.

Olina (Hawaiian) filled with happiness.

Olivia (Latin) olive tree. (English) a form of Olga.

Ondine (Latin) little wave.

Ophelia (Greek) helper.

Oprah (Hebrew) runaway.

Paige (English) young child.

Pamela (Greek) honey.

Paola (Italian) a form of Paula.

Paris (French) the capital of France.

Patience (English) patient.

Patrice (French) a form of Patricia.

Patricia (Latin) noble-woman. A feminine form of Patrick.

Paula (Latin) small. A feminine form of Paul.

Paulette (Latin) a familiar form of Paula.

Pauline (Latin) a familiar form of Paula.

Pearl (Latin) jewel.

Peggy (Greek) a familiar form of Margaret.

Penny (Greek) weaver.

Petra (Greek, Latin) small rock. A feminine form of Peter.

Philippa (Greek) lover of horses. A feminine form of Philip.

Phoebe (Greek) shining.

Phylicia (Greek) a form of Felicia. (Latin) fortunate; happy.

Phyllis (Greek) green bough.

Piper (English) pipe player.

Polly (Latin) a familiar form of Paula.

Porsche (German) a form of Portia.

Portia, Porsha (Latin) offering.

Precious (French) precious, dear.

Princess (English) daughter of royalty.

Priscilla (Latin) ancient.

Priya (Hindi) beloved; sweet natured.

Qadira (Arabic) powerful.

Queisha (American) a combination of the prefix Qu + Aisha.

Questa (French) searcher.

Quiana (American) a combination of the prefix Qu + Anna.

Quincy (Irish) fifth.

Quinella (Latin) an alternate form of Quintana.

Quinn (German, English) queen.

Quintana (Latin) fifth. (English) queen's lawn. A feminine form of Quintin.

Rachel, Rachael (Hebrew) female sheep.

Rachelle (French) a form of Rachel.

Racquel, Raquel (French) forms of Rachel.

Rae (English) doe. (Hebrew) a short form of Rachel.

Raeann (American) a combination of Rae + Ann.

Raina (German) mighty. (English) a short form of Regina.

Ramona (Spanish) mighty; wise protector.

Randall (English) protected.

Randy, Randi (English) familiar forms of Miranda, Randall.

Rashida (Swahili, Turkish) righteous.

Raven (English) blackbird.

Rayna (Scandinavian) mighty. (Yiddish) pure, clean. (French) a familiar form of Lorraine. (English) king's advisor. A feminine form of Reynold.

Reanna (German, English) an alternate form of Raina. (American) an alternate form of Raeann.

Reba (Hebrew) fourth-born child. A short form of Rebecca.

Rebecca, Rebekah (Hebrew) tied, bound.

Reena (Greek) peaceful.

Regan (Irish) little ruler.

Regina (Latin) queen. (English) king's advisor. A feminine form of Reginald.

Reina (Spanish) a short form of Regina.

Rena (Hebrew) song; joy. A familiar form of Irene, Regina, Sabrina, Serena.

Renata, Renita (French) an alternate form of Renee.

Rene (Greek) a short form of Irene, Renee.

Renee, Renae (French) born again.

Reva (Latin) revived. (Hebrew) rain; one-fourth. An alternate form of Reba.

Reyna (Greek) peaceful. (English) an alternate form of Reina.

Rhea (Greek) brook, stream.

Rhiannon (Welsh) witch; nymph; goddess.

Rhoda (Greek) from Rhodes, an island off of Greece.

Rhonda, Ronda (Welsh) grand.

Richelle (German, French) rich and powerful ruler. A feminine form of Richard.

Ricki, Rikki (American) familiar forms of Erica.

Riley (Irish) valiant.

Rita (Sanskrit) brave; honest. (Greek) a short form of Margarita.

Roberta (English) famous brilliance. A feminine form of Robert.

Robin, Robyn (English) robin. Alternate forms of Roberta.

Rochelle (Hebrew) an alternate form of Rachel. (French) large stone.

Rocio (Spanish) dewdrops.

Rosa (Italian, Spanish) a form of Rose.

Rosalie (English) a form of Rosalind.

Rosalind, Rosalyn (Spanish) fair rose.

Rosanna, Roseanna (English) combinations of Rose + Anna.

Rosanne, Roseanne (English) combinations of Rose + Ann.

Rose (Latin) rose.

Rosemarie (English) a combination of Rose + Marie.

Rosemary (English) a combination of Rose + Mary.

Rosetta (Italian) a form of Rose.

Roxana, Roxann, Roxanna, Roxanne (Persian) sunrise.

Ruby (French) precious stone.

Ruth (Hebrew) friendship.

Ryan (Irish) little ruler.

Sabina (Latin) from the Sabine, a tribe in ancient Italy.

Sable (English) sable; sleek.

Sabra (Hebrew) thorny cactus fruit.

Sabrina (Latin) boundary line. (Hebrew) a familiar form of Sabra. (English) princess.

Sade (Hebrew) an alternate form of Sarah, Shardae.

Sadie (Hebrew) a familiar form of Sarah.

Safiya (Arabic) pure; serene; best friend.

Salena (French) solemn; dignified.

Sally (English) a familiar form of Sarah.

Samantha (Aramaic) listener. (Hebrew) told by God.

Samara (Latin) elm-tree seed.

Sana (Arabic) mountaintop; splendid; brilliant.

Sandeep (Punjabi) enlightened.

Sandi (Greek) a familiar form of Sandra.

Sandra (Greek) a short form of Alexandra, Cassandra.

Sandy (Greek) a familiar form of Cassandra, Sandra.

Santana (Spanish) saint.

Sarah, Sara (Hebrew) princess.

Sari (Hebrew) a familiar form of Sarah. (Arabic) noble.

Sarina (Hebrew) a familiar form of Sarah.

Sarita (Hebrew) a familiar form of Sarah.

Sasha, Sacha (Russian) short forms of Alexandra.

Saundra (English) a form of Sandra.

Savannah (Spanish) treeless plain.

Scarlett (English) bright red.

Selena, Selina (Greek) moon.

Serena (Latin) peaceful.

Shaina (Yiddish) beautiful.

Shakia (American) a combination of the prefix Sha + Kia.

Shakira (Arabic) thankful. A feminine form of Shakir.

Shakita, Shaquita (American) combinations of the prefix Sha + Kita.

Shalana (American) a combination of the prefix Sha + Lana.

Shalonda (American) a combination of the prefix Sha + Ondine.

Shameka (American) a combination of the prefix Sha + Meka.

Shamika (American) a combination of the prefix Sha + Mika.

Shamira (Hebrew) precious stone.

Shana, Shauna, Shawna (Hebrew) God is gracious. (Irish) forms of Jane.

Shanae (Irish) an alternate form of Shana.

Shanda, Shandra (American) forms of Chanda, Shana.

Shandi (English) a familiar form of Shana.

Shaneka, Shanika (American) combinations of the prefix Sha + Nika.

Shanel, Shanell, Shanelle (American) forms of Chanel.

Shani (Swahili) marvelous.

Shanita (American) a combination of the prefix Sha + Nita.

Shanna (Irish) an alternate form of Shana, Shannon.

Shannon (Irish) small and wise.

Shanta, Shantae, Shante (French) alternate forms of Chantal.

Shantel, Shantell (American) forms of Chantal.

Shara (Hebrew) a short form of Sharon.

Sharaya (Hebrew) an alternate form of Sarah.

Shardae, Sharday (Punjabi) charity. (Yoruba) honored by royalty. (Arabic) runaway.

Sharee (English) a form of Shari.

Shari (French) an alternate form of Cherie. (Hungarian) a form of Sarah.

Sharita (French) a familiar form of Shari. (American) a form of Charity.

Sharla (French) a short form of Sharlene.

Sharlene (French) a form of Charlene.

Sharon (Hebrew) desert plain. An alternate form of Sharaya.

Shatara (Hindi) umbrella. (Arabic) good; industrious. (American) a combination of Sharon + Tara.

Shaunda (Irish) an alternate form of Shana.

Shavonne (American) a combination of the prefix Sha + Yvonne.

Shawnda (Irish) an alternate form of Shana.

Shay, Shae, Shea (Irish) fairy palace.

Shayla (Irish) an alternate form of Shay.

Shayna (Hebrew) a form of Shaina.

Sheena (Hebrew) God is gracious. (Irish) a form of Jane.

Sheila (Latin) blind. (Irish) a form of Cecelia.

Shelby (English) ledge estate.

Shelly, Shelley (English) meadow on the ledge. (French) familiar forms of Michelle.

Shena (Irish) an alternate form of Sheena.

Shera (Aramaic) light.

Sherell (French) an alternate form of Cheryl, Sheryl.

Sherika (Punjabi) relative. (Arabic) easterner.

Sherita (French) a form of Sherry, Sheryl.

Sherry, Sheree, Sheri, Sherri (French) alternate forms of Shari.

Sheryl (French) an alternate form of Cheryl. A familiar form of Shirley.

Shilo (Hebrew) God's gift.

Shira (Hebrew) song.

Shirley (English) bright meadow.

Shona, Shonda (Irish) forms of Jane. Alternate forms of Shana.

Shoshana (Hebrew) an alternate form of Susan.

Shyla (English) an alternate form of Sheila.

Sierra (Irish) black. (Spanish) saw-toothed.

Silvia, Sylvia (Latin) forest.

Simone (Hebrew) she heard. (French) a feminine form of Simon.

Siobhan (Irish) a form of Joan.

Skye (Arabic) water giver. (Dutch) a short form of Skyler.

Skyler (Dutch) sheltering.

Sommer (English) summer; summoner. (Arabic) black.

Sondra (Greek) a short form of Alexandra.

Sonia (Russian, Slavic) an alternate form of Sonya.

Sonja (Scandinavian) a form of Sonya.

Sonya (Greek) wise. (Russian, Slavic) a form of Sophia.

Sophia, Sofia (Greek) wise.

Sophie (Greek) a familiar form of Sophia.

Stacey, Stacy (Greek) resurrection. (Irish) short forms of Anastasia, Natasha.

Staci (Greek) an alternate form of Stacey.

Stacia (English) a short form of Anastasia.

Starr (English) star.

Stella (Latin) star. (French) a familiar form of Estelle.

Stephanie, Stefanie, Stephenie (Greek) crowned. Feminine forms of Stephan.

Stevie (Greek) a familiar form of Stephanie.

Stormy (English) impetuous by nature.

Sue (Hebrew) a short form of Susan.

Summer (English) summertime.

Sunny (English) bright; cheerful.

Sunshine (English) sunshine.

Susan, Susanna, Susannah (Hebrew) lily.

Susie (American) a familiar form of Susan.

Suzanne (English) a form of Susan.

Suzette (French) a form of Susan.

Sybil (Greek) prophet.

Sydney (French) from Saint Denis, France. A feminine form of Sidney.

Sylvana (Latin) forest.

Syreeta (Hindi) good traditions. (Arabic) companion.

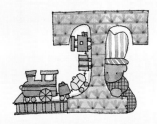

Tabitha, Tabatha (Greek, Aramaic) gazelle.

Takia (Arabic) worshiper.

Talia (Greek) blooming. (Hebrew) dew from heaven. (Latin, French) birthday.

Tamar (Hebrew) a short form of Tamara. (Russian) a twelfth-century Georgian queen.

Tamara, Tamra (Hebrew) palm tree.

Tameka (Aramaic) twin.

Tamika (Japanese) child of the people.

Tamila (American) a combination of the prefix Ta + Mila.

Tammie, Tammi (English) alternate forms of Tammy.

Tammy (Hebrew) a familiar form of Tamara. (English) twin.

Tana (Slavic) a short form of Tanya.

Taneisha, Tanesha, Tanisha (American) combinations of the prefix Ta + Niesha.

Tania (Russian, Slavic) a form of Tanya.

Tanis, Tannis (Slavic) forms of Tania.

Tanya (Russian, Slavic) a short form of Tatiana.

Tara (Aramaic) throw; carry. (Irish) rocky hill. (Arabic) a measurement.

Tarra (Irish) an alternate form of Tara.

Taryn (Irish) an alternate form of Tara.

Tasha (Greek) born on Christmas day. (Russian) a short form of Natasha.

Tashia (Slavic) a form of Tasha. (Hausa) a bird in flight.

Tasia (Slavic) a familiar form of Tasha.

Tatiana (Slavic) fairy queen.

Tatum (English) cheerful.

Tavia (Latin) a short form of Octavia.

Tawny (Gypsy) little one. (English) brownish yellow, tan.

Tawnya (American) a combination of Tawny + Tonya.

Taylor (English) tailor.

Tegan (Welsh) beautiful, attractive.

Tenesha, Tenisha (American) combinations of the prefix Te + Niesha.

Tennille (American) a combination of the prefix Te + Nellie.

Tera, Terra (Latin) earth. (Japanese) swift arrow.

Terri, Teri, Terry (Greek) familiar forms of Theresa.

Terri-Lynn (American) a combination of Terri + Lynn.

Tess (Greek) a short form of Theresa.

Tessa (Greek) a short form of Theresa.

Thanh (Vietnamese) bright blue. (Punjabi) good place.

Thao (Vietnamese) respectful of parents.

Thea (Greek) goddess.

Theresa, Teresa, Therese (Greek) reaper.

Thi (Vietnamese) poem.

Tia (Greek) princess. (Spanish) aunt.

Tiana (Greek) princess. (Latin) a short form of Tatiana.

Tiara (Latin) crowned.

Tierney (Irish) noble.

Tiffanie, Tiffani (Latin) alternate forms of Tiffany.

Tiffany (Greek) God's appearance. (Latin) trinity.

Tina (Spanish, American) a short form of Martina, Christina, Valentina.

Tisha (Latin) a short form of Leticia.

Toni (Greek, Latin) a short form of Antoinette, Antonia.

Tonia (Latin, Slavic) an alternate form of Toni, Tonya.

Tonya (Slavic) fairy queen.

Tori (Japanese) bird. (English) an alternate form of Tory.

Tory (Latin) a short form of Victoria. (English) victorious.

Tosha (Punjabi) armaments. (Polish) a familiar form of Antonia. (Russian) an alternate form of Tasha.

Toya (Spanish) a form of Tory.

Tracey, Tracy (Greek) familiar forms of Theresa. (Latin) warrior.

Tracie, Traci (Latin) alternate forms of Tracey.

Tressa (Greek) a short form of Theresa.

Trice (Greek) a short form of Theresa.

Tricia (Latin) an alternate form of Trisha.

Trina (Greek) a short form of Katrina. (Hindi) points of sacred kusa grass.

Trisha (Latin) a familiar form of Patricia. (Hindi) thirsty.

Trista (Latin) a short form of Tristen.

Tristen (Latin) bold. A feminine form of Tristan.

Trudy (German) beloved warrior.

Twyla (English) woven of double thread.

Tyesha (American) a combination of the prefix Ty + Aisha.

Tyler (English) tailor.

Tyra (Scandinavian) battler.

Ulrica (German) wolf ruler; ruler of all.

Urika (Omaha) useful to everyone.

Urit (Hebrew) bright.

Ursula (Greek) little bear.

Vail (English) valley.

Val (Latin) a short form of Valentina, Valerie.

Valencia (Spanish) strong.

Valene (Latin) a short form of Valentina.

Valentina (Latin) strong.

Valera (Russian) a form of Valerie.

Valerie, Valarie (Latin) strong.

Vanessa (Greek) butterfly.

Vanna (Greek) a short form of Vanessa. (Cambodian) golden.

Veanna (American) a combination of the prefix Ve + Anna.

Vera (Latin) true. (Slavic) faith. A short form of Veronica.

Verity (Latin) truthful.

Verna (Latin) springtime.

Veronica (Latin) true image.

Veronique (French) a form of Veronica.

Vicky, Vicki (Latin) familiar forms of Victoria.

Victoria (Latin) victorious.

Violet (French) a plant with purplish blue flowers.

Virginia (Latin) pure, virginal.

Vita (Latin) life.

Vivian, Viviana (Latin) full of life.

Wainani (Hawaiian) beautiful water.

Wakeisha (American) a combination of the prefix Wa + Keisha.

Walker (English) cloth; walker.

Wanda (German) wanderer.

Wendy, Wendi (Welsh) white; light skinned. Familiar forms of Gwendolyn, Wanda.

Whitney (English) white island.

Willow (English) willow tree.

Winifred (German) peaceful friend.

Winona (Lakota) oldest daughter.

Winter (English) winter.

Wynne (Welsh) white; light skinned.

Xandra (Greek) an alternate form of Zandra. (Spanish) a short form of Alexandra.

Xanthe (Greek) yellow; blond.

Xaviera (Basque) owner of the new house. (Arabic) bright. A feminine form of Xavier.

Xenia (Greek) hospitable.

Xiang (Chinese) fragrant.

Xuan (Vietnamese) spring.

Xuxa (Portuguese) a familiar form of Susan.

Yasmin, Yasmine (Persian) alternate forms of Jasmine.

Yesenia (Arabic) flower.

Yoko (Japanese) good girl.

Yolanda (Greek) violet flower.

Yuri (Japanese) lily.

Yvette (French) a familiar form of Yvonne.

Yvonne (French) young archer. (Scandanavian) yew wood; bow wood.

Zabrina (American) an alternate form of Sabrina.

Zacharie (Hebrew) God remembered. A feminine form of Zachariah.

Zahar (Hebrew) daybreak, dawn.

Zandra (Greek) an alternate form of Sandra.

Zara (Hebrew) an alternate form of Sarah, Zora.

Zelene (English) sunshine.

Zelia (Spanish) sunshine.

Zena (Greek) an alternate form of Xenia. (Ethiopian) news. (Persian) woman.

Zina (Greek) an alternate form of Xenia, Zena. (African) secret spirit. (English) hospitable.

Zita (Spanish) rose. (Arabic) mistress. A short form of names ending in "sita" or "zita."

Zoe, Zoey (Greek) life.

Zora (Slavic) aurora, dawn.

Zudora (Sanskrit) laborer.

Zuri (Basque) white; light skinned. (Swahili) beautiful.

Boys' Names

Aaron (Hebrew) enlightened. (Arabic) messenger.

Abdul (Arabic) servant.

Abdullah (Arabic) servant of Allah.

Abel (Hebrew) breath. (Assyrian) meadow. (German) a short form of Abelard.

Abelard (German) noble; resolute.

Abraham (Hebrew) father of many nations.

Abram (Hebrew) a short form of Abraham.

Adam (Phoenician) man; mankind. (Hebrew) earth; man of the red earth.

Addison (English) son of Adam.

Adham (Arabic) black.

Adrian (Greek) rich. (Latin) dark.

Adriel (Hebrew) member of God's flock.

Adrien (French) a form of Adrian.

Ahmad, Ahmed (Arabic) most highly praised.

Aidan (Irish) fiery.

Ajay (Punjabi) victorious; invincible. (American) a combination of the initials A. + J.

Akeem (Hebrew) God will establish.

Alain (French) a form of Alan.

Alan, Allan, Allen (Irish) handsome; peaceful.

Albert (German, French) noble and bright.

Alberto (Italian) a form of Albert.

Alden (English) old; wise protector.

Aldo (Italian) old; elder.

Alec, Alex (Greek) short forms of Alexander.

Alejandro (Spanish) a form of Alexander.

Alessandro (Italian) a form of Alexander.

Alexander (Greek) defender of mankind.

Alexandre (French) a form of Alexander.

Alexis (Greek) a short form of Alexander.

Alfonso (Italian, Spanish) a form of Alphonse.

Alfred (English) elf counselor; wise counselor.

Alfredo (Italian, Spanish) a form of Alfred.

Ali (Arabic) greatest. (Swahili) exalted.

Alonzo (Spanish) a form of Alphonse.

Alphonse (German) noble and eager.

Alphonso (Italian) a form of Alphonse.

Alton (English) old town.

Alvaro (Spanish) just; wise.

Alvin (Latin) white; light skinned. (German) friend to all; noble friend; friend of elves.

Amandeep (Punjabi) light of peace.

Amar (Punjabi) immortal. (Arabic) builder.

Amir (Hebrew) proclaimed. (Punjabi) wealthy; king's minister. (Arabic) prince.

Amit (Punjabi) unfriendly. (Arabic) highly praised.

Ammon (Egyptian) hidden.

Amos (Hebrew) burdened, troubled.

Anders (Swedish) a form of Andrew.

Andre (French) a form of Andrew.

Andreas (Greek) an alternate form of Andrew.

Andres (Spanish) a form of Andrew.

Andrew (Greek) strong; manly; courageous.

Andy (Greek) a short form of Andrew.

Angel (Greek) angel. (Latin) messenger.

Angelo (Italian) a form of Angel.

Angus (Scottish) exceptional, outstanding.

Anibal (Phoenician) grace of God.

Anson (German) divine. (English) Ann's son.

Anthony (Greek) flourishing. (Latin) praiseworthy.

Antoine (French) a form of Anthony.

Anton (Slavic) a form of Anthony.

Antonio (Italian) a form of Anthony.

Antony (Latin) an alternate form of Anthony.

Antwan (Arabic) a form of Anthony.

Archie (German) bold. (English) bowman.

Ari (Hebrew) a short form of Ariel.

Aric (German) an alternate form of Richard. (Scandinavian) an alternate form of Eric.

Ariel (Hebrew) lion of God.

Arlen (Irish) pledge.

Armand (Latin, German) an alternate form of Herman.

Armando (Spanish) a form of Armand.

Arnold (German) eagle ruler.

Aron, Arron (Hebrew) alternate forms of Aaron.

Arthur (Irish) noble; lofty hill. (Scottish) bear. (English) rock. (Icelandic) follower of Thor.

Arturo (Italian) a form of Arthur.

Asher (Hebrew) happy; blessed.

Ashley (English) ash-tree meadow.

Ashton (English) ash-tree settlement.

Aubrey (German) noble; bearlike.

August (Latin) a short form of Augustus.

Augustus (Latin) majestic; venerable.

Austin (Latin) a short form of Augustus.

Avery (English) a form of Aubrey.

Axel (Latin) axe. (German) small oak tree; source of life.

Baron (German, English) nobleman; baron.

Barrett (German) strong as a bear.

Barry (Welsh) son of Harry. (Irish) spear; marksman. (French) gate; fence.

Bart (Hebrew) a short form of Barton.

Barton (English) barley farm; Bart's town.

Basil (Greek, Latin) royal; kingly.

Beau (French) handsome.

Ben (Hebrew) a short form of Benjamin.

Benito (Italian) blessed.

Benjamin (Hebrew) son of my right hand.

Bennett (Latin) little blessed one.

Benny (Hebrew) a familiar form of Benjamin.

Benoit (French) a form of Benito. (English) a yellow, flowering rose plant.

Benson (Hebrew) son of Ben.

Benton (English) Ben's town; town on the moors.

Bernard (German) brave as a bear.

Bert (German, English) bright; shining.

Bilal (Arabic) chosen.

Bill (German) a short form of William.

Billy (German) a familiar form of Bill, William.

Bjorn (Scandinavian) a form of Bernard.

Blaine (Irish) thin, lean. (English) river source.

Blair (Irish) plain, field. (Welsh) place.

Blaise (Latin) stammerer. (English) flame; trail mark made on a tree.

Blake (English) attractive; dark.

Blayne (Irish) an alternate form of Blaine.

Bo (English) a form of Beau.

Bob (English) a short form of Robert.

Bobby (English) a familiar form of Bob, Robert.

Boyd (Scottish) yellow haired.

Brad (English) a short form of Bradford, Bradley.

Braden (English) broad valley.

Bradford (English) broad river crossing.

Bradley, Bradly (English) broad meadow.

Brady (Irish) spirited. (English) broad island.

Branden (English) beacon valley.

Brandon (English) beacon hill.

Brant, Brandt (English) proud.

Braxton (English) Brock's town.

Braydon (English) broad hill.

Breck (Irish) freckled.

Brendan, Brennan, Brennen (Irish) little raven. (English) sword.

Brenden (Irish) an alternate form of Brendan.

Brent (English) a short form of Brenton.

Brenton (English) steep hill.

Bret, Brett, Brit, Britt (Scottish) from Great Britain.

Brian (Irish, Scottish) strong; virtuous; honorable.

Brice (Welsh) alert; ambitious. (English) son of Rice.

Brock (English) badger.

Broderick (Welsh) son of the famous ruler. (English) broad ridge.

Brody, Brodie (Irish) ditch; canal builder.

Bronson (English) son of Brown.

Brook (English) brook, stream.

Brooks (English) son of Brook.

Brown (English) brown; bear.

Bruce (French) brushwood thicket; woods.

Bruno (German, Italian) brown haired; brown skinned.

Bryan, Bryant (Irish) alternate forms of Brian.

Bryce (Welsh) an alternate form of Brice.

Bryon (German) cottage. (English) bear.

Bryson (Welsh) son of Brice.

Buddy (English) herald, messenger.

Byron (French) cottage. (English) barn.

Cade (Welsh) battler.

Cale (Hebrew) a short form of Caleb.

Caleb (Hebrew) dog; faithful. (Arabic) bold, brave.

Calvin (Latin) bald.

Camden (Scottish) winding valley.

Cameron (Scottish) crooked nose.

Carey (Greek) pure. (Welsh) castle; rocky island.

Carl (German, English) a form of Charles. A short form of Carlton.

Carlin (Irish) little champion.

Carlo (Italian) a form of Carl, Charles.

Carlos (Spanish) a form of Carl, Charles.

Carlton (English) Carl's town.

Carmelo (Hebrew) vineyard; garden.

Carmine (Latin) song; crimson. (Italian) a form of Carmelo.

Carr (Scandinavian) marsh.

Carson (English) son of Carr.

Carter (English) cart driver.

Casey (Irish) brave.

Cassidy (Irish) clever; curly haired.

Cecil (Latin) blind.

Cedric (English) battle chieftain.

Cerek (Greek) an alternate form of Cyril. (Polish) lordly.

Cesar (Spanish) long haired.

Chad (English) warrior. A short form of Chadwick.

Chadwick (English) warrior's town.

Chance (English) a short form of Chauncey.

Chandler (English) candle maker.

Channing (English) wise. (French) canon; church official.

Charles (German) farmer. (English) strong and manly.

Charlie (German, English) a familiar form of Charles.

Chase (French) hunter.

Chauncey (English) chancellor; church official.

Chaz (English) a familiar form of Charles.

Chester (English) fortress.

Chet (English) a short form of Chester.

Chris (Greek) a short form of Christian, Christopher.

Christian, Cristian (Greek) follower of Christ; anointed.

Christophe (French) a form of Christopher.

Christopher, Cristopher (Greek) Christ bearer.

Clarence (Latin) clear; victorious.

Clark (French) cleric; scholar.

Claude (Latin, French) lame.

Claudio (Italian) a form of Claude.

Clay (English) clay pit. A short form of Clayton.

Clayton (English) town built on clay.

Clement (Latin) merciful.

Cliff (English) a short form of Clifford, Clifton.

Clifford (English) cliff at the river crossing.

Clifton (English) cliff town.

Clint (English) a short form of Clinton.

Clinton (English) hill town.

Clyde (Welsh) warm. (Scottish) a river in Scotland.

Cody, Codey (English) cushion.

Colby (English) dark; dark haired.

Cole (Greek) a short form of Nicholas. (Latin) cabbage farmer. (English) a short form of Coleman.

Coleman (Latin) cabbage farmer. (English) coal miner.

Colin (Greek) a short form of Nicholas. (Irish) young cub.

Collin (Scottish) a form of Colin, Collins.

Collins (Greek) son of Colin. (Irish) holly.

Colt (English) young horse; frisky. A short form of Colter, Colton.

Colter (English) herd of colts.

Colton (English) coal town.

Connor (Irish) praised; exalted. (Scottish) wise.

Conor (Irish) an alternate form of Connor.

Conrad (German) brave counselor.

Cooper (English) barrel maker.

Corbin (Latin) raven.

Cordell (French) rope maker.

Cordero (Spanish) little lamb.

Corey (Irish) hollow.

Cornelius (Greek) cornel tree. (Latin) horn colored.

Cornell (French) a form of Cornelius.

Corry (Latin) a form of Corey.

Cortez (Spanish) conqueror.

Cory (Latin) a form of Corey. (French) a familiar form of Cornell.

Coty (French) slope, hillside.

Courtland (English) court's land.

Courtney (English) from the court.

Coy (English) woods.

Craig (Irish, Scottish) crag, steep rock.

Cullen (Irish) handsome.

Curt (Latin) a short form of Courtney, Curtis.

Curtis (Latin) enclosure. (French) courteous.

Cyril (Greek) lordly.

Cyrus (Persian) sun.

Dakota (Dakota) friend; partner; tribal name.

Dale (English) dale, valley.

Dallas (Scottish) a town in Scotland; a city in Texas.

Dalton (English) town in the valley.

Damian, Damien, Damion (Greek) tamer; soother.

Damon (Greek) constant; loyal. (Latin) spirit; demon.

Dan (Hebrew) a short form of Daniel. (Vietnamese) yes.

Dana (Scandinavian) from Denmark.

Dane (English) from Denmark.

Daniel, Danial, Daniele (Hebrew) God is my judge.

Danny (Hebrew) a familiar form of Daniel.

Dante (Latin) lasting, enduring.

Darcy (Irish) dark. (French) from Arcy, France.

Darell (English) a form of Darrell.

Daren (Irish) an alternate form of Darren. (Hausa) born at night.

Darin, Daron (Irish) alternate forms of Darren.

Darius (Greek) wealthy.

Darnell (English) hidden place.

Darren (Irish) great. (English) small; rocky hill.

Darwin (English) dear friend.

Daryl, Darrell, Darryl, Derrell (French) darling, beloved; grove of oak trees.

Dave (Hebrew) a short form of David, Davis.

David (Hebrew) beloved.

Davin (Scandinavian) brilliant Finn.

Davis (Welsh) son of David.

Davon (American) a form of Davin.

Dawson (English) son of David.

Dayne (Scandinavian) a form of Dane.

Dayton (English) day town; bright, sunny town.

Dean (French) leader. (English) valley.

Deandre (French) a combination of the prefix De + Andre.

Deangelo (Italian) a combination of the prefix De + Angelo.

Dejuan (American) a combination of the prefix De + Juan.

Delbert (English) bright as day.

Delvin (English) proud friend; friend from the valley.

Demarco (Italian) a combination of the prefix De + Marco.

Demarcus (American) a combination of the prefix De + Marcus.

Demario (Italian) a combination of the prefix De + Mario.

Demetrius, Demetris, Dimitrios (Greek) lover of the earth.

Dennis, Denis (Greek) a follower of Dionysus, the god of wine.

Denny (Greek) a familiar form of Dennis.

Denver (English) green valley.

Deon (Greek) an alternate form of Dennis.

Derek, Darrick, Derick, Derrick (German) ruler of the people.

Deron (Hebrew) bird; freedom. (American) a combination of the prefix De + Ron.

Deshawn (American) a combination of the prefix De + Shawn.

Desmond (Irish) from Munster, Ireland.

Deven (Hindi) for God. (Irish) an alternate form of Devin.

Devin, Devon (Irish) poet.

Dewayne (Irish) an alternate form of Dwayne. (American) a combination of the prefix De + Wayne.

Dewey (Welsh) prized.

Dexter (Latin) dexterous, adroit. (English) fabric dyer.

Diego (Spanish) a form of Jacob, James.

Dillon (Irish) loyal, faithful.

Dimitri (Russian) a form of Demetrius.

Dino (German) little sword. (Italian) a form of Dean.

Dion (Greek) a short form of Dennis.

Dirk (German) a short form of Derek.

Domenico (Italian) a form of Dominic.

Dominic, Dominick (Latin) belonging to the Lord.

Dominique (French) a form of Dominic.

Don (Scottish) a short form of Donald.

Donald (Scottish) world leader; proud ruler.

Donnell (Irish) brave; dark.

Donnie, Donny (Irish) familiar forms of Donald.

Donovan (Irish) dark warrior.

Dontae, Donté (American) forms of Dante.

Dorian (Greek) from Doris, Greece.

Douglas (Scottish) dark river, dark stream.

Doyle (Irish) dark stranger.

Drake (English) dragon; owner of the inn with the dragon trademark.

Drew (Welsh) wise. (English) a short form of Andrew.

Duncan (Scottish) brown warrior.

Durell (Scottish, English) king's doorkeeper.

Dustin (German) valiant fighter. (English) brown rock quarry.

Dusty (English) a familiar form of Dustin.

Dustyn (English) an alternate form of Dustin.

Dwayne, Duane (Irish) dark.

Dwight (English) blond.

Dylan (Welsh) sea.

Earl (Irish) pledge. (English) nobleman.

Eddie, Eddy (English) familiar forms of Edgar, Edward.

Edgar (English) successful spearman.

Edmund, Edmond (English) prosperous protector.

Eduardo (Spanish) a form of Edward.

Edward (English) prosperous guardian.

Edwin (English) prosperous friend.

Efrain (Hebrew) fruitful.

Elam (Hebrew) highlands.

Eldon (English) holy hill.

Eli (Hebrew) uplifted. A short form of Elijah, Elisha.

Elias (Greek) a form of Elijah.

Elijah (Hebrew) the Lord is my God.

Elisha (Hebrew) God is my salvation.

Elliot, Elliott (English) forms of Eli, Elijah.

Ellis (English) a form of Elias.

Elmer (English) noble; famous.

Elton (English) old town.

Elvin (English) a form of Alvin.

Elvis (Scandinavian) wise.

Emerson (German, English) son of Emery.

Emery, Emory (German) industrious leader.

Emil (Latin) flatterer. (German) industrious.

Emilio (Italian, Spanish) a form of Emil.

Emmanuel, Emanuel (Hebrew) God is with us.

Emmett (German) industrious; strong. (English) ant.

Enrique (Spanish) a form of Henry.

Eric (German) a short form of Frederick. (Scandinavian) ruler of all. (English) brave ruler.

Erich (Czech, German) a form of Eric.

Erik (Scandinavian) an alternate form of Eric.

Erin (Irish) peaceful.

Ernest, Earnest (English) earnest, sincere.

Ernesto (Spanish) a form of Ernest.

Errol (Latin) wanderer. (English) an alternate form of Earl.

Ervin, Erwin (English) sea friend.

Esteban (Spanish) a form of Stephen.

Ethan (Hebrew) strong; firm.

Eugene (Greek) born to nobility.

Evan (Irish) young warrior. (English) a form of John.

Everett (German) courageous as a boar.

Ezekiel (Hebrew) strength of God.

Ezra (Hebrew) helper; strong.

Fabian (Latin) bean grower.

Fabio (Latin) an alternate form of Fabian.

Farley (English) bull meadow; sheep meadow.

Felipe (Spanish) a form of Philip.

Felix (Latin) fortunate; happy.

Ferdinand (German) daring, adventurous.

Fernando (Spanish) a form of Ferdinand.

Fletcher (English) arrow featherer; arrow maker.

Floyd (English) a form of Lloyd.

Forrest, Forest (French) forest; woodsman.

Francesco (Italian) a form of Francis.

Francis (Latin) free; from France.

Francisco (Portuguese, Spanish) a form of Francis.

François (French) a form of Francis.

Frank (English) a short form of Francis, Franklin.

Frankie (English) a familiar form of Frank.

Franklin, Franklyn (English) free landowner.

Fraser (French) strawberry. (English) curly haired.

Fred (German) a short form of Frederick.

Freddie (German) a familiar form of Frederick.

Frederick, Fredrick (German) peaceful ruler.

Fritz (German) a familiar form of Frederick.

Gabriel (Hebrew) devoted to God.

Galen (Greek) healer; calm. (Irish) little and lively.

Gareth (Welsh) gentle.

Garrett, Garett (Irish) brave spearman.

Garrison (French) garrison, troops stationed at a fort.

Garry (English) an alternate form of Gary.

Garth (Scandinavian) garden; gardener. (Welsh) a short form of Gareth.

Gary (German) mighty spearman. (English) a familiar form of Gerald.

Gavin (Welsh) white hawk.

Gene (Greek) a short form of Eugene.

Geoffrey (English) a form of Jeffrey.

George (Greek) farmer.

Gerald (German) mighty spearman.

Gerard (English) brave spearman.

Gerardo (Spanish) a form of Gerard.

Gerrit (Dutch) a form of Gerald.

Gerry (English) a familiar form of Gerald, Gerard.

Giancarlo (Italian) a combination of John + Charles.

Gideon (Hebrew) tree cutter.

Gilbert (English) brilliant pledge; trustworthy.

Gilberto (Spanish) a form of Gilbert.

Gilles (French) goatskin shield.

Gino (Greek) a familiar form of Eugene. (Italian) a short form of names ending in "gene," "gino."

Giovanni (Italian) a form of John.

Giuseppe (Italian) a form of Joseph.

Glenn, Glen (Irish) woody valley, glen.

Gordon (English) triangular hill.

Grady (Irish) noble; illustrious.

Graeme (Scottish) a form of Graham.

Graham (English) grand home.

Grant (English) great; giving.

Grayson (English) bailiff's son.

Greg, Gregg (Latin) short forms of Gregory.

Gregory, Greggory (Latin) vigilant watchman.

Griffin (Latin) hooked nose.

Guillaume (French) a form of William.

Guillermo (Spanish) a form of William.

Gurpreet (Punjabi) devoted to the guru; devoted to the Prophet.

Gustave (Scandinavian) staff of the Goths.

Gustavo (Italian, Spanish) a form of Gustave.

Guy (Hebrew) valley. (German) warrior. (French) guide.

Hakim (Arabic) wise. (Ethiopian) doctor.

Hank (American) a familiar form of Henry.

Hans (Scanadinavian) a form of John.

Hardeep (Punjabi) an alternate form of Harpreet.

Harlan (English) hare's land; army land.

Harley (English) hare's meadow; army meadow.

Harold (Scandinavian) army ruler.

Harpreet (Punjabi) loves God; devoted to God.

Harris (English) a short form of Harrison.

Harrison (English) son of Harry.

Harry (English) a familiar form of Harold.

Harvey (German) army warrior.

Hassan (Arabic) handsome.

Hayden (English) hedged valley.

Heath (English) heath.

Hector (Greek) steadfast.

Henry (German) ruler of the household.

Herbert (German) glorious soldier.

Heriberto (Spanish) a form of Herbert.

Herman (Latin) noble. (German) soldier.

Hiram (Hebrew) noblest; exalted.

Homer (Greek) hostage; pledge; security.

Horace (Latin) keeper of the hours.

Houston (English) hill town.

Howard (English) watch-man.

Hubert (German) bright mind; bright spirit.

Hugh (English) a short form of Hubert.

Hugo (Latin) a form of Hugh.

Humberto (German) brilliant strength.

Hunter (English) hunter.

Huy (Vietnamese) glorious.

Ian, Iain (Scottish) forms of John.

Ibrahim (Arabic) a form of Abraham. (Hausa) my father is exalted.

Imran (Arabic) host.

Ira (Hebrew) watchful.

Irvin (Irish, Welsh, English) a short form of Irving.

Irving (Irish) handsome. (Welsh) white river. (English) sea friend.

Isaac (Hebrew) he will laugh.

Isaiah (Hebrew) God is my salvation.

Ismael (Hebrew) God will hear.

Israel (Hebrew) prince of God; wrestled with God.

Ivan (Russian) a form of John.

J (American) an initial used as a first name.

Jace, Jayce (American) combinations of the initials J. + C.

Jack (American) a familiar form of Jacob, John.

Jackie (American) a familiar form of Jack.

Jackson (English) son of Jack.

Jacob, Jakob (Hebrew) supplanter; substitute.

Jacques (French) a form of Jacob, James.

Jade (Spanish) jade; precious stone.

Jaime (Spanish) a form of Jacob, James.

Jake (Hebrew) a short form of Jacob.

Jamal, Jamaal, Jamel, Jamil (Arabic) handsome.

Jamar (American) a form of Jamal.

James (Hebrew) supplanter; substitute. (English) a form of Jacob.

Jameson, Jamison (English) son of James.

Jamie, Jamye (English) familiar forms of James.

Jan (Dutch, Slavic) a form of John.

Jared, Jarrod, Jarryd, Jered (Hebrew) descendant.

Jarell (Scandinavian) a form of Gerald.

Jaron (Hebrew) he will sing; he will cry out.

Jarrell, Jerel, Jerrell (English) forms of Gerald.

Jarrett (English) a form of Garrett, Jared.

Jarvis (German) skilled with a spear.

Jason, Jayson (Greek) healer.

Jaspal (Punjabi) living a virtuous lifestyle.

Jasper (French) green ornamental stone.

Javan, Javon (Hebrew) son of Japheth in the Bible.

Javaris (English) a form of Jarvis.

Javier (Spanish) owner of a new house.

Jay (French) blue jay. (English) a short form of James, Jason.

Jaymes (English) an alternate form of James.

Jean (French) a form of John.

Jed (Hebrew) a short form of Jedidiah. (Arabic) hand.

Jedidiah (Hebrew) friend of God; beloved of God.

Jeff (English) a short form of Jefferson, Jeffrey. A familiar form of Geoffrey.

Jefferson (English) son of Jeff.

Jeffrey, Jeffery, Jeffry (English) divinely peaceful.

Jerald (English) a form of Gerald.

Jeramie, Jeramy, Jeremey, Jeremie (Hebrew) alternate forms of Jeremy.

Jeremiah (Hebrew) God will uplift.

Jeremy, Jermey (English) forms of Jeremiah.

Jermaine (English) sprout, bud.

Jerome, Jeromy (Latin) holy.

Jeron (English) a form of Jerome.

Jerrard (French) a form of Gerard.

Jerry (German) mighty spearman. (English) a familiar form of Gerald, Gerard.

Jess (Hebrew) a short form of Jesse.

Jesse, Jessie (Hebrew) wealthy.

Jesus (Hebrew) an alternate form of Joshua.

Jim (Hebrew) supplanter; substitute. (English) a short form of James.

Jimmy, Jimmie (English) alternate forms of Jim.

Joachim (Hebrew) God will establish.

Joaquin (Spanish) a form of Joachim.

Jody (Hebrew) a familiar form of Joseph.

Joe (Hebrew) a short form of Joseph.

Joel (Hebrew) God is willing.

Joey (Hebrew) a familiar form of Joe, Joseph.

John (Hebrew) God is gracious.

Johnny, Johnnie (Hebrew) familiar forms of John.

Johnson (English) son of John.

Jon (Hebrew) an alternate form of John. A short form of Jonathan.

Jonah (Hebrew) dove.

Jonas (Lithuanian) a form of John. (Hebrew) he accomplishes.

Jonathan, Johnathan, Johnathon, Jonathon (Hebrew) gift of God.

Jordan, Jordon (Hebrew) descending.

Jordy, Jory (Hebrew) familiar forms of Jordan.

Jorge (Spanish) a form of George.

Jose (Spanish) a form of Joseph.

Josef (German, Portuguese, Czech, Scandinavian) a form of Joseph.

Joseph (Hebrew) God will add, God will increase.

Josh (Hebrew) a short form of Joshua.

Joshua (Hebrew) God is my salvation.

Josiah (Hebrew) fire of the Lord.

Josue (Hebrew) an alternate form of Joshua.

Jovan (Latin) Jove-like; majestic. (Slavic) a form of John.

Jr (Latin) a short form of Junior.

Juan (Spanish) a form of John.

Judd (Hebrew) praised.

Jude (Latin) a form of Judd.

Judson (English) son of Judd.

Julian (Greek, Latin) an alternate form of Julius.

Julien (Latin) an alternate form of Julian.

Julio (Hispanic) a form of Julius.

Julius (Greek, Latin) youthful; downy bearded.

Junior (Latin) young.

Justin, Justyn (Latin) just; righteous.

Kacey (Irish) an alternate form of Casey. (American) a combination of the initials K. + C.

Kade (Scottish) wetlands. (American) a combination of the initials K. + D.

Kai (Welsh) keeper of the keys. (Hawaiian) sea.

Kale (Hawaiian) a familiar form of Carl.

Kaleb (Hebrew) an alternate form of Caleb.

Kalen, Kalin (Arabic) alternate forms of Kale. (Irish) alternate forms of Kellen.

Kalvin (Latin) an alternate form of Calvin.

Kameron (Scottish) an alternate form of Cameron.

Kane (Welsh) beautiful. (Irish) tribute. (Japanese) golden. (Hawaiian) eastern sky.

Kareem, Karim (Arabic) noble; distinguished.

Karl (German) an alternate form of Carl.

Kasey (Irish) an alternate form of Casey.

Kayle (Hebrew) faithful dog.

Keaton (English) where hawks fly.

Keegan (Irish) little; fiery.

Keenan (Irish) little Keene.

Keene (German) bold; sharp. (English) smart.

Keith (Welsh) forest. (Scottish) battle place.

Kellen (Irish) mighty warrior.

Kelly (Irish) warrior.

Kelsey (Scandinavian) island of ships.

Kelvin (Irish, English) narrow river.

Ken (Japanese) one's own kind. (Scottish) a short form of Kendall, Kendrick, Kenneth.

Kendall (English) valley of the river Kent.

Kendrick (Irish) son of Henry. (Scottish) royal chieftain.

Kenneth (Irish) handsome. (English) royal oath.

Kenny (Scottish) a familiar form of Kenneth.

Kent (Welsh) white; bright. (English) a short form of Kenton.

Kenton (English) from Kent, England.

Kentrell (English) king's estate.

Keon (Irish) a form of Evan.

Kerry (Irish) dark; dark haired.

Kevin, Kevan, Keven (Irish) handsome.

Khalid (Arabic) eternal.

Khalil (Arabic) friend.

Kieran (Irish) little and dark.

Kim (Greek) hollow vessel. (English) warrior chief.

Kirby (Scandinavian) church village. (English) cottage by the water.

Kirk (Scandinavian) church.

Kody (English) an alternate form of Cody.

Kolby (English) an alternate form of Colby.

Konrad (German) a form of Conrad.

Korey, Kory (Irish) alternate forms of Corey.

Kraig (Irish, Scottish) an alternate form of Craig.

Kris (Greek) an alternate form of Chris. A short form of Kristian, Kristopher.

Kristian (Greek) an alternate form of Christian.

Kristofer (Swedish) a form of Kristopher.

Kristoph (French) a form of Kristopher.

Kristopher (Greek) an alternate form of Christopher.

Kurt (Latin, German, French) a short form of Kurtis. An alternate form of Curt.

Kurtis (Latin, French) an alternate form of Curtis.

Kyle, Kiel, Kyele (Irish) narrow piece of land; place where cattle graze. (Yiddish) crowned with laurels.

Kyler (English) a form of Kyle.

Lamar (German) famous throughout the land. (French) sea, ocean.

Lamont (Scandinavian) lawyer.

Lance (Latin) light spear. (German) land.

Landon, Landen (English) open, grassy meadow.

Lane, Layne (English) narrow road.

Lanny (American) a familiar form of Laurence.

Laron (French) thief.

Larry (Latin) a familiar form of Lawrence.

Lars (Scandinavian) a form of Lawrence.

Laurence, Lawrence (Latin) crowned with laurel.

Lazaro (Hebrew) God has helped.

Lee, Leigh (English) short forms of Farley and names containing "lee."

Leif (Scandinavian) beloved.

Leland (English) meadow-land; protected land.

Leo (Latin) lion.

Leon (Greek, German) a short form of Leonard.

Leonard (German) brave as a lion.

Leonardo (Italian) a form of Leonard.

Leonel (English) little lion.

Leroy (French) king.

Leslie (Scottish) gray fortress.

Lester (Latin) chosen camp. (English) from Leicester, England.

Levi (Hebrew) joined in harmony.

Lewis (English) a form of Louis.

Liam (Irish) a form of William.

Lincoln (English) settlement by the pool.

Lindsay, Lindsey (English) linden-tree island.

Lionel (French) lion cub.

Lloyd (Welsh) gray haired; holy.

Logan (Irish) meadow.

Lonnie (German, Spanish) a familiar form of Alonzo.

Loren (Latin) a short form of Laurence.

Lorenzo (Italian, Spanish) a form of Laurence.

Lorne (Latin) a short form of Laurence.

Louis (German) famous warrior.

Lowell (French) young wolf. (English) beloved.

Luc (French) a form of Luke.

Lucas (German, Irish, Danish, Dutch) a form of Lucius.

Lucius (Latin) light; bringer of light.

Luigi (Italian) a form of Louis.

Luis (Spanish) a form of Louis.

Lukas (Greek, Czech, Swedish) a form of Luke.

Luke (Latin) a form of Lucius.

Luther (German) famous warrior.

Lyle (French) island.

Lyndon (English) linden-tree hill.

Lynn (English) waterfall; brook.

Mack (Scottish) a short form of names beginning with "Mac" and "Mc."

Mackenzie (Irish) son of the wise leader.

Madison (English) son of Maud; good son.

Malachi (Hebrew) angel of God.

Malcolm (Scottish) follower of Saint Columba, an early Scottish saint. (Arabic) dove.

Malik (Arabic) a form of Malachi. (Punjabi) lord, master.

Mandeep (Punjabi) mind full of light.

Manuel (Hebrew) a short form of Emmanuel.

Marc (French) a form of Mark.

Marcel (French) a form of Marcus.

Marcello (Italian) a form of Marcus.

Marco (Italian) a form of Marcus.

Marcos (Spanish) a form of Marcus.

Marcus, Markus (Latin) martial, warlike.

Mario (Italian) a form of Marion.

Marion (French) bitter; sea of bitterness. A masculine form of Mary.

Mark (Latin) a short form of Marcus.

Marko (Latin) an alternate form of Marco, Mark.

Marlin (English) deep-sea fish.

Marlon (French) a form of Merlin.

Marques (Portuguese) nobleman.

Marquis (French) nobleman.

Marshall (French) caretaker of the horses; military title.

Martell (English) hammerer.

Martin (Latin) martial, warlike.

Marty (Latin) a familiar form of Martin.

Marvin (English) lover of the sea.

Mason (French) stoneworker.

Massimo (Italian) greatest.

Mathieu (French) a form of Matthew.

Matt (Hebrew) a short form of Matthew.

Matthew, Mathew (Hebrew) gift of God.

Maurice (Latin) dark skinned; moor; marshland.

Mauricio (Spanish) a form of Maurice.

Max (Latin) a short form of Maximilian, Maxwell.

Maxime (French) most excellent.

Maximilian (Latin) greatest.

Maxwell (English) great spring.

Mckay (Scottish) son of the rejoicing man.

Melvin (Irish) armored chief. (English) mill friend; council friend.

Merle (French) famous.

Merlin (English) falcon.

Mervin (Irish) a form of Marvin.

Micah (Hebrew) an alternate form of Michael.

Michael, Mikal (Hebrew) who is like God?

Micheal, Mikeal (Irish) forms of Michael.

Michel (French) a form of Michael.

Michele (Italian) a form of Michael.

Mickey (Irish) a familiar form of Michael.

Miguel (Portuguese, Spanish) a form of Michael.

Mikael (Swedish) a form of Michael.

Mike (Hebrew) a short form of Michael.

Mikel (Basque) a form of Michael.

Mikhail (Greek, Russian) a form of Michael.

Miles (Greek) millstone. (Latin) soldier. (German) merciful. (English) a short form of Michael.

Milton (English) mill town.

Mitch (English) a short form of Mitchell.

Mitchell (English) a form of Michael.

Moises (Portuguese, Spanish) a form of Moses.

Monroe (Irish) the mouth of the Roe River.

Monte (Latin) mountain.

Montez (Spanish) dweller in the mountains.

Montgomery (English) rich man's mountain.

Monty (English) a form of Monte.

Morgan (Scottish) sea warrior.

Morris (Latin) dark skinned; moor; marshland. (English) a form of Maurice.

Moses (Hebrew) drawn out of the water. (Egyptian) son, child.

Moshe (Hebrew, Polish) an alternate form of Moses.

Muhammad, Mohammad, Mohammed (Arabic) praised.

Murray (Scottish) sailor.

Mustafa (Arabic) chosen; royal.

Myles (Latin) soldier. (German) an alternate form of Miles.

Myron (Greek) fragrant ointment.

Nathan, Nathen (Hebrew) short forms of Nathaniel.

Nathanie (Hebrew) a familiar form of Nathaniel.

Nathaniel, Nathanael, Nathanial (Hebrew) gift of God.

Neil, Neal (Irish) champion.

Nelson (English) son of Neil.

Nevin (Irish) worshiper of the saint. (English) middle; herb.

Nicholas (Greek) victorious people.

Nick (English) a short form of Dominic, Nicholas.

Nicklaus, Nickolas, Nikolas (Greek) alternate forms of Nicholas.

Nicola, Nicolas (Italian) forms of Nicholas.

Nigel (Latin) dark night.

Noah (Hebrew) peaceful; restful.

Noel (French) day of Christ's birth.

Nolan (Irish) famous; noble.

Norman (French) Norseman.

Oliver (Latin) olive tree. (Scandinavian) kind; affectionate.

Olivier (French) a form of Oliver.

Omar (Arabic) highest; follower of the Prophet. (Hebrew) reverent.

Oren (Hebrew) pine tree. (Irish) light skinned; white.

Orlando (German) famous throughout the land. (Spanish) a form of Roland.

Orry (Latin) from the Orient.

Oscar (Scandinavian) divine spearman.

Osvaldo (Spanish) a form of Oswald.

Oswald (English) God's power; God's crest.

Otis (Greek) keen of hearing. (German) son of Otto.

Otto (German) rich.

Owen (Irish) born to nobility; young warrior. (Welsh) a form of Evan.

Pablo (Spanish) a form of Paul.

Paolo (Italian) a form of Paul.

Paris (Greek) lover.

Parker (English) park keeper.

Pascal (French) born on Easter or Passover.

Pasquale (Italian) a form of Pascal.

Patrick (Latin) nobleman.

Paul (Latin) small.

Paulo (Portuguese, Swedish, Hawaiian) a form of Paul.

Payton (English) warrior's town.

Pedro (Spanish) a form of Peter.

Percy (French) prisoner of the valley.

Perry (English) a familiar form of Peter.

Pete (English) a short form of Peter.

Peter (Greek, Latin) small rock.

Philip, Phillip (Greek) lover of horses.

Philippe (French) a form of Philip.

Pierce (English) a form of Peter.

Pierre (French) a form of Peter.

Pierre-Luc (French) a combination of Pierre + Luc.

Pietro (Italian) a form of Peter.

Preston (English) priest's estate.

Prince (Latin) chief; prince.

Quentin (Latin) fifth. (English) queen's town.

Quincy (French) fifth son's estate.

Quinn (Irish) a short form of Quincy, Quintin.

Quintin, Quinton (Latin) alternate forms of Quentin.

Rafael (Spanish) a form of Raphael.

Raheem (Punjabi) compassionate God.

Rahim (Arabic) merciful.

Rahul (Arabic) traveler.

Ralph (English) wolf counselor.

Ramon (Spanish) a form of Raymond.

Ramsey (English) ram's island.

Rand (English) shield; warrior.

Randal, Randall, Randolph (English) shield-wolf.

Randy (English) a familiar form of Rand, Randal.

Raphael (Hebrew) God has healed.

Rashad (Arabic) wise counselor.

Rashawn (American) a combination of the prefix Ra + Shawn.

Rasheen (American) a combination of the prefix Ra + Sean.

Raul (French) a form of Ralph.

Ravi (Hindi) sun.

Ray (French) kingly; royal. (English) a short form of Raymond.

Raymond (English) mighty; wise protector.

Raynard (French) wise; bold, courageous.

Reece, Reese (Welsh) enthusiastic; stream.

Regan (Irish) little king.

Reggie (English) a familiar form of Reginald.

Reginald, Reginal (English) king's advisor.

Regis (Latin) regal.

Reid, Reed (English) red-head.

Reinaldo (Spanish) a form of Reginald.

Remi (French) from Rheims, France.

Rene (French) reborn.

Reuben, Ruben (Hebrew) behold a son.

Rex (Latin) king.

Reynold (English) king's advisor.

Rhett (Welsh) an alternate form of Rhys.

Rhys (Welsh) an alternate form of Reece.

Ricardo (Portuguese, Spanish) a form of Richard.

Rice (Welsh) an alternate form of Reece. (English) rich; noble.

Richard (English) rich and powerful ruler.

Rick (German) a short form of Richard.

Ricky, Rickey (English) familiar forms of Richard, Rick.

Rico (Spanish) a familiar form of Richard.

Riley (Irish) valiant.

Robbie, Robby (English) familiar forms of Robert.

Robert (English) famous brilliance.

Roberto (Portuguese, Spanish) a form of Robert.

Robin (English) a short form of Robert.

Rocco (Italian) rock.

Rocky (American) a familiar form of Rocco.

Roderick, Rodrick (German) famous ruler.

Rodney (English) island clearing.

Rodolfo (Spanish) a form of Rudolph.

Rodrigo (Italian, Spanish) a form of Roderick.

Roger, Rodger (German) famous spearman.

Roland (German) famous throughout the land.

Rolando (Portuguese, Spanish) a form of Roland.

Roman (Latin) from Rome.

Ron (Hebrew) a short form of Aaron, Ronald.

Ronald (Scottish) a form of Reginald.

Ronnie (Scottish) a familiar form of Ronald.

Roosevelt (Dutch) rose field.

Rory (German) a familiar form of Roderick. (Irish) red king.

Roscoe (Scandinavian) deer forest.

Ross (Latin) rose. (Scottish) peninsula. (French) red.

Roy (French) king. A short form of Royce.

Royce (English) son of Roy.

Rudolph (German) famous wolf.

Rudy (English) a familiar form of Rudolph.

Rufus (Latin) redhead.

Russell (French) redhead; fox colored.

Rusty (French) a familiar form of Russell.

Ryan, Rian, Ryne (Irish) little king.

Rylan (English) land where rye is grown.

Salvador (Spanish) savior.

Salvatore (Italian) savior.

Sam (Hebrew) a short form of Samuel.

Samir (Arabic) entertaining companion.

Sammy (Hebrew) a familiar form of Samuel.

Samson (Hebrew) like the sun.

Samuel (Hebrew) heard God; asked of God.

Sandeep (Punjabi) enlightened.

Sandy (English) a familiar form of Alexander.

Santiago (Spanish) a form of James.

Sasha (Russian) a short form of Alexander.

Saul (Hebrew) asked for; borrowed.

Sawyer (English) wood worker.

Schuyler (Dutch) sheltering.

Scott (English) from Scotland.

Scotty (English) a familiar form of Scott.

Seamus (Irish) a form of James.

Sean (Hebrew) God is gracious. (Irish) a form of John.

Sebastian (Greek) venerable. (Latin) revered.

Sebastien (French) form of Sebastian.

Serge (Latin) attendant.

Sergio (Italian) a form of Serge.

Seth (Hebrew) appointed.

Shad (Punjabi) happy-go-lucky.

Shakir (Arabic) thankful.

Shane, Shayne (Irish) alternate forms of Sean.

Shannon (Irish) small and wise.

Sharif (Arabic) honest; noble.

Shavar (Hebrew) comet.

Shawn, Shaun (Irish) alternate forms of Sean.

Shea (Irish) courteous.

Shelby (English) ledge estate.

Sheldon (English) farm on the ledge.

Shepherd (English) shepherd.

Sherman (English) sheep shearer; resident of a shire.

Sidney (French) from Saint Denis, France.

Silas (Latin) forest dweller.

Simeon (French) a form of Simon.

Simon (Hebrew) he heard.

Skyler, Skylar (Dutch) alternate forms of Schuyler.

Solomon (Hebrew) peaceful.

Sonny (English) a familiar form of Grayson, Madison.

Spencer, Spenser (English) dispenser of provisions.

Stacey, Stacy (Greek) productive. (Latin) stable; calm.

Stanley (English) stony meadow.

Stefan (German, Polish, Swedish) a form of Stephen.

Stefano (Italian) a form of Stephen.

Steffen (Norwegian) a form of Stephen.

Stephane (French) a form of Stephen.

Stephen, Stephan, Stephon (Greek) crowned.

Sterling (English) valuable; silver penny.

Steve (Greek) a short form of Stephen, Steven.

Steven (Greek) an alternate form of Stephen.

Stevie (English) a familiar form of Stephen, Steven.

Stuart, Stewart (English) caretaker, steward.

Sundeep (Punjabi) light; enlightened.

Syed (Arabic) happy.

Sylvain (French) a form of Sylvester.

Sylvester (Latin) forest dweller.

Tad (Greek, Latin) a short form of Thaddeus. (Welsh) father.

Tai (Vietnamese) weather; prosperous; talented.

Talon (French, English) claw, nail.

Tanner (English) leather worker, tanner.

Tariq (Arabic) conqueror.

Tate (Scandinavian, English) cheerful. (Native American) long-winded talker.

Taurean (Latin) strong; forceful.

Tavaris (Aramaic) misfortune.

Taylor (English) tailor.

Ted (English) a short form of Edward, Theodore.

Teddy (English) a familiar form of Edward, Theodore.

Terrell, Terell, Terrel (German) thunder ruler.

Terrence, Terence, Terrance (Latin) smooth.

Terry (English) a familiar form of Terrence.

Thaddeus (Greek) courageous. (Latin) praiser.

Theo (English) a short form of Theodore.

Theodore (Greek) gift of God.

Theron (Greek) hunter.

Thomas (Greek, Aramaic) twin.

Tim (Greek) a short form of Timothy.

Timmy (Greek) a familiar form of Timothy.

Timothy (Greek) honoring God.

Titus (Greek) giant. (Latin) hero.

Tobias (Hebrew) God is good.

Toby (Hebrew) a familiar form of Tobias.

Todd (English) fox.

Tom (English) a short form of Thomas.

Tomas (German) a form of Thomas.

Tommy, Tommie (Hebrew) familiar forms of Thomas.

Tony (Greek) flourishing. (Latin) praiseworthy. (English) a short form of Anthony.

Torrence (Latin) an alternate form of Terrence. (Irish) knolls.

Tory, Torrey (English) familiar forms of Torrence.

Trace (Irish) an alternate form of Tracy.

Tracy (Greek) harvester. (Latin) courageous. (Irish) battler.

Travis (English) crossroads.

Tremaine, Tremayne (Scottish) house of stone.

Trent (Latin) torrent, rapid stream. (French) thirty.

Trenton (Latin) town by the rapid stream.

Trevor (Irish) prudent. (Welsh) homestead.

Trey (English) three; third.

Tristan (Welsh) bold.

Troy (Irish) foot soldier. (French) curly haired. (English) water.

Tuan (Vietnamese) goes smoothly.

Tucker (English) fuller, tucker of cloth.

Ty (English) a short form of Tyler, Tyrone.

Tyler, Tylor (English) tile maker.

Tyree (Scottish) island dweller.

Tyrel, Tyrell (American) forms of Terrell.

Tyron (American) a form of Tyrone.

Tyrone (Greek) sovereign. (Irish) land of Owen.

Tyson (French) son of Ty.

Ulysses (Latin) wrathful.

Upton (English) upper town.

Uriah (Hebrew) my light.

Uriel (Hebrew) God is my light.

Valere (Latin, French) strong; healthy.

Van (Dutch) a short form of Vandyke.

Vance (English) thresher.

Vandyke (Dutch) dike.

Vaughn (Welsh) small.

Vernon (Latin) springlike; youthful.

Vicente (Spanish) a form of Vincent.

Victor (Latin) victor, conqueror.

Vijay (Hindi) victorious.

Vince (English) a short form of Vincent.

Vincent (Latin) victor, conqueror.

Vincenzo (Italian) a form of Vincent.

Virgil (Latin) rod bearer, staff bearer.

Vito (Italian) a form of Victor.

Vladimir (Russian) famous prince.

Wade (English) ford, river crossing.

Wallace (English) from Wales, England.

Walter (German) army ruler, general. (English) woodsman.

Warren (German) general; warden; rabbit hutch.

Waylon (English) land by the road.

Wayne (English) wagon maker.

Wendell (German) wanderer. (English) good dale, good valley.

Wesley, Westley (English) western meadow.

Weston (English) western town.

Whitney (English) white island; white water.

Wilbert (German) brilliant; resolute.

Wilfred (German) determined peacemaker.

Wilfredo (Spanish) a form of Wilfred.

Will (English) a short form of William.

Willard (German) determined and brave.

William (English) determined guardian.

Willie (German) a familiar form of William.

Willis (German) son of Willie.

Wilson (English) son of Will.

Winston (English) friendly town; victory town.

Wyatt (French) little warrior.

Xan (Greek) a short form of Alexander.

Xander (Greek) a short form of Alexander.

Xanthus (Latin) golden haired.

Xavier (Basque) owner of the new house. (Arabic) bright.

Xerxes (Persian) ruler.

Yakov (Russian) a form of Jacob.

Yevgenyi (Russian) a form of Eugene.

Yusuf (Arabic, Swahili) a form of Joseph.

Yves (French) young archer.

Zachariah, Zacharia, Zechariah, (Hebrew) God remembered.

Zachary, Zachery, Zackary, Zackery (Hebrew) familiar forms of Zachariah.

Zane (English) a form of John.